Cambridge Elements ⸗

Elements in Publishing and Book Culture
edited by
Samantha J. Rayner
University College London
Leah Tether
University of Bristol

THE BRICK-AND-MORTAR BOOKSTORE IN CONTEMPORARY INDIA

Nayantara Srinivasan
University of Münster

Shaftesbury Road, Cambridge CB2 8EA, United Kingdom

One Liberty Plaza, 20th Floor, New York, NY 10006, USA

477 Williamstown Road, Port Melbourne, VIC 3207, Australia

314–321, 3rd Floor, Plot 3, Splendor Forum, Jasola District Centre,
New Delhi – 110025, India

103 Penang Road, #05–06/07, Visioncrest Commercial, Singapore 238467

Cambridge University Press is part of Cambridge University Press & Assessment,
a department of the University of Cambridge.

We share the University's mission to contribute to society through the pursuit of
education, learning and research at the highest international levels of excellence.

www.cambridge.org
Information on this title: www.cambridge.org/9781009591201

DOI: 10.1017/9781009591232

© Nayantara Srinivasan 2025

This publication is in copyright. Subject to statutory exception and to the provisions
of relevant collective licensing agreements, no reproduction of any part may take place
without the written permission of Cambridge University Press & Assessment.

When citing this work, please include a reference to the DOI 10.1017/9781009591232

First published 2025

A catalogue record for this publication is available from the British Library

ISBN 978-1-009-59120-1 Paperback
ISSN 2514-8524 (online)
ISSN 2514-8516 (print)

Cambridge University Press & Assessment has no responsibility for the persistence
or accuracy of URLs for external or third-party internet websites referred to in this
publication and does not guarantee that any content on such websites is, or will remain,
accurate or appropriate.

For EU product safety concerns, contact us at Calle de José Abascal, 56, 1°, 28003
Madrid, Spain, or email eugpsr@cambridge.org

The Brick-and-Mortar Bookstore in Contemporary India

Elements in Publishing and Book Culture

DOI: 10.1017/9781009591232
First published online: August 2025

Nayantara Srinivasan
University of Münster

Author for correspondence: Nayantara Srinivasan, ntara13@gmail.com

ABSTRACT: This Element explores the landscape of anglophone trade bookselling in India, aiming to identify some key factors that have influenced the changing place of the brick-and-mortar bookstore over the last decade. The discussion focuses on a specific time period identified as a significant turning point, the advent of the COVID-19 pandemic. The pandemic led to a series of developments in the field of Indian publishing: a newly emerging body of public discourse within the industry, highlighting the persistent marginalisation faced by brick-and-mortar bookstores; the temporary weakening of Amazon's near-monopoly; and bookstores' growing use of online platforms for sales, publicity, and activism. Drawing upon a range of primary sources and case studies, this Element explores how these developments altered what John B. Thompson calls 'the logic of the field' of contemporary Indian bookselling, transforming the brick-and-mortar bookstore into a newly revitalised space with possibilities for further expansion, growth, and diversity.

KEYWORDS: bookselling, bookstores, India, publishing studies, book studies

© Nayantara Srinivasan 2025

ISBNs: 9781009591201 (PB), 9781009591232 (OC)
ISSNs: 2514-8524 (online), 2514-8516 (print)

Contents

1	Introduction	1
2	Brick-and-Mortar Bookselling in Contemporary India	10
3	Bookselling and the Pandemic: A Transformation in the Field	24
4	Bookselling in the Pandemic: Independent Bookseller Activism	42
5	New Field, New Logics: The Brick-and-Mortar Bookstore in Post-Pandemic India	54
6	Conclusion	69
	Bibliography	74

1 Introduction

In 2015, *Fortune India* published an article titled 'The death of the bookstore', mourning the fact that bookshops in India were 'rapidly becom[ing] an endangered species' thanks to shop closures, shrinking store space, and a new 'online-offline war' in retail.[1] The 'death of the bookstore' was a familiar refrain in India throughout the 2010s, as newspapers reported 'the sudden collapse of bookshops and book retailing' across the country.[2] Nor did the booksellers quoted in these articles provide any note of optimism: Janaki Viswanath, for example, saw 'the death of small bookshops as inevitable in the sea of changes',[3] and Ajay Mago, owner of the chain Om Book Shops, had an even more dire prediction: 'Five years from now, there will be no bookshops.'[4]

Mago made his prediction in 2015 – two years after Amazon had launched operations in India, disrupting the brick-and-mortar book trade. Five years later, the onset of COVID-19, with its devastating effects for physical retail worldwide, appeared to be another nail in the coffin. But in 2023, when Amazon India celebrated its tenth anniversary, it did so amidst a somewhat surprising bookselling landscape. Social media was alive with information about bookshop events, and newspapers now spoke of bookstores in terms of expansion and reinvention, rather than death.[5] Crossword – India's leading bookstore chain, whose store space had shrunk dramatically between 2004 and 2015 – was now poised to expand to over 300

---

[1] Kaavya Chandrasekaran, 'The death of the bookstore', *Fortune India*, 5 July 2015.

[2] Binoo K. John, 'Why bookshops are closing down when book-reading is thriving', *Scroll*, 7 August 2015. See also, for instance, 'The death of Mumbai's Strand Book Stall', *Rediff*, 2 March 2018; Soma Ghosh, 'On the death of a neighbour', *The Times of India*, 10 July 2014; Abhay Vaidya, 'The death of a bookstore: Why Pune's Twistntales is closing down', *Firstpost*, 23 February 2013.

[3] Vaidya, 'The death of a bookstore'.

[4] Chandrasekaran, 'The death of the bookstore'.

[5] See, for instance, Rashmi Menon, 'Indie bookstores are turning the page', *Mint*, 8 October 2020; Faizan Haidar, 'Bookstores look to turn the page, expand outlets', *Economic Times*, 12 January 2023.

outlets 'in the next few years'.[6] And Ajay Mago, who had been prepared for his industry to become obsolete, opened a new branch of his bookstore in December 2023.[7]

What factors might have contributed to this revival of the bookstore in India, and what does this mean for the place of brick-and-mortar bookselling in the wider field of trade publishing? This Element explores the landscape of contemporary anglophone bookselling in India, aiming to identify some of the key elements and structures that have influenced the changing place of the brick-and-mortar bookstore over the last decade. To do so, I focus on a specific time period identified as a significant turning point, the advent of the COVID-19 pandemic. The pandemic led to a series of unexpected consequences and developments in the field of Indian publishing: among others, a newly emerging body of public discourse within the industry, highlighting the challenges faced by brick-and-mortar bookstores; the temporary weakening of Amazon's position as a result of pandemic restrictions; and bookstores' growing use of social media and online platforms for sales, publicity, and activism. I argue that these factors, taken together, have significantly affected what John B. Thompson refers to as 'the logic of the field'[8] of contemporary bookselling in India, and explain the transformation of the brick-and-mortar bookstore from a marginalised position within trade publishing to a newly revitalised space with possibilities for further expansion, growth, and diversity.

The idea of 'the death of the bookstore' is, of course, not new to discussions of bookselling; bookselling in the long twenty-first century is often spoken of specifically in terms of its volatility, as a space of 'seismic changes' from the point of view of publishers as well as readers.[9] In the

---

[6] Chandrasekaran, 'The death of the bookstore'; Haidar, 'Bookstores look to turn the page'.

[7] Om Book Shop (ombookshop), 'Our first ever book shop in West Delhi', Instagram, 22 December 2023.

[8] John B. Thompson, *Merchants of Culture: The Publishing Business in the Twenty-First Century* (Newark: Polity Press, 2013).

[9] Judith Rosen, 'The changing world of bookselling', *Publishers Weekly*, 19 April 2022.

primary anglophone markets, the UK and the United States, these transformations often refer to two key time periods: the era of the chain bookstore as a main player in retail in the late 1990s, to the detriment of independent bookstores; and the period after the entrance, and eventual monopoly, of Amazon, 'the world's largest and most powerful bookshop'.[10] 'Seismic changes' could, in fact, be said to apply to contemporary publishing as a whole; Ted Striphas argues that the instability and dynamism of the publishing landscape is a fundamental characteristic of the 'late age of print', as a 'period rife with consistency and contradiction, tradition and transformation, deference and discord'.[11] Notwithstanding these changes, and the threat to physical bookstores, however, bookselling continues to be a valuable business: as of 2017, the 'worldwide market value' for books was around 122 billion euro, with seven countries contributing to roughly 70% of the market: 'the USA, China, Germany, the UK, Japan, France, and India'.[12]

Despite both its current economic value and its long cultural history – book retail and distribution form a vital component of the earliest models of publishing and the circulation of books, from Darnton's communication circuit to Adams and Barker's 'cycle of the book'[13] – bookselling has long remained relatively underrepresented in book and publishing studies scholarship. Writing in 2006, Audrey Laing and Jo Royle note that while bookshops are vital to 'cultural life', '[b]ookselling in particular has no significant body of academic research which investigates either the

---

[10] Niels Peter Thomas, 'Bookselling', in *The Oxford Handbook of Publishing*, eds. Angus Phillips and Michael Bhaskar (Oxford: Oxford University Press, 2019), 399.

[11] Ted Striphas, *The Late Age of Print: Everyday Book Culture from Consumerism to Control* (New York: Columbia University Press, 2009), 175–6.

[12] Thomas, 'Bookselling', 399.

[13] Robert Darnton, 'What is the history of books?', *Daedalus* 111, no. 3 (1982): 65–83; Thomas R. Adams and Nicolas Barker, 'A new model for the study of the book', in *The Book History Reader*, eds. David Finkelstein and Alistair McCleery, 2nd ed. (London: Routledge, 2006), 47–65.

commercial or cultural implications of the trade'.[14] Recent years have seen increasing scholarship on bookselling, predominantly on the primary anglophone markets of the United States and the UK. While John B. Thompson, Ted Striphas, and Greco et al. all discuss changes in patterns of book retail as part of their examinations of contemporary trade publishing, a growing body of work focuses on the brick-and-mortar bookstore in particular, from the place of independent and radical bookstores to considerations of the spatiality and imaginary of the bookstore.[15] Helena Markou and Audrey Laing, among others, have analysed patterns of physical bookselling in individual book markets such as the UK and Scotland; and the post-pandemic years have seen explorations of the effects of COVID-19 on physical and online retail in specific territories including the UK, Australia, and Vietnam.[16] Within this emerging body of research, however, work on

---

[14] Audrey Laing and Jo Royle, 'Bookselling culture and consumer behaviour: Marketing strategies and consumer responses in UK chain bookshops', in *The Future of the Book in the Digital Age*, eds. Bill Cope and Angus Phillips (Oxford: Chandos Publishing, 2006), 116.

[15] Thompson, *Merchants of Culture*; Striphas, *The Late Age of Print*; Albert N. Greco, Clara E. Rodríguez, and Robert M. Wharton, *The Culture and Commerce of Publishing in the 21st Century* (Stanford: Stanford University Press, 2007). For work on bookselling see, for instance, Eben J. Muse, *Fantasies of the Bookstore* (Cambridge: Cambridge University Press, 2022); Kristen Doyle Highland, *The Spaces of Bookselling: Stores, Streets, and Pages* (Cambridge: Cambridge University Press, 2023); Josh Cook, *The Art of Libromancy: Selling Books and Reading Books in the Twenty-first Century* (Windsor: Biblioasis, 2023).

[16] See, for example, Helena Markou, 'The window of opportunity: Success and failure in UK bookselling', *Logos* 34, no. 1 (September 2023): 7–23; Audrey Laing, 'Indies in Scotland: Exploring the unique role of independent bookshops in Scotland's towns and villages', *Publishing Research Quarterly* 36, no. 4 (December 2020): 585–600; Claire Squires, 'Essential? different? exceptional? the book trade and Covid-19', *C21 Literature: Journal of 21st-Century Writings* 9, no. 1 (2022); Kenna MacTavish, 'Crisis book browsing: Restructuring the retail shelf life of books', in *Bookshelves in the Age of the COVID-19 Pandemic*, eds. Corinna Norrick-Rühl and Shafquat Towheed (Cham: Springer International, 2022), 49–68; Hoang Viet Nguyen, Hiep Xuan Tran, Le Van Huy

bookselling in India is almost non-existent. English-language publishing in India is a subject of scholarship, particularly from a post-colonial perspective, but discussions of bookselling tend to be restricted to histories of individual bookstores.[17] More recent work by Kanupriya Dhingra and Pritha Mukherjee focuses on 'informal' bookselling spaces such as the book bazaar, a unique and under-researched facet of the country's bookselling landscape.[18] However, there continues to be no extended or comprehensive research on brick-and-mortar bookstores in the country, whether historical or contemporary – despite their undeniable influence on the wider context of Indian publishing.

While it would be out of the scope of this Element to construct a history of brick-and-mortar bookselling in the country, focusing on the current landscape can tell us much about the past, present, and possible future of the bookstore in contemporary India. Simone Murray suggests that the goal of contemporary publishing studies is to 'demonstrate the rich research potential of current developments, investigating the influence and interdependence' of institutions and individuals within the book trade.[19] In this vein, I focus on a set of developments in Indian bookselling between March 2020 and March 2024, adopting a mixed methods approach that combines textual analysis with case studies of specific bookstores.

Section 2 provides a brief overview of brick-and-mortar bookselling in contemporary India, focusing particularly on the twin phenomena of the 'death of the bookstore' and the rise of Amazon. My analysis then focuses on two main sets of primary data in Sections 3 and 4. First, Section 3

et al., 'Online book shopping in Vietnam: The impact of the COVID-19 pandemic situation', *Publishing Research Quarterly* 36, no. 3 (September 2020): 437–45.

[17] See, for instance, Milinda De, 'Sarat Book House: Bookselling, a noble profession', *Logos* 33, no. 2–3 (December 2022): 69–73.

[18] Kanupriya Dhingra, *Old Delhi's Parallel Book Baẓaar* (Cambridge: Cambridge University Press, 2024); see also Kanupriya Dhingra and Pritha Mukherjee, 'Bookselling in India: The "proper" and the "parallel"', presentation as part of the Bookselling Research Network, 26 January 2024.

[19] Simone Murray, 'Publishing studies: Critically mapping research in search of a discipline', *Publishing Research Quarterly* 22, no. 4 (December 2006): 16.

examines a significant body of public discourse in India, that itself emerged as a direct response to the pandemic: the online series 'Publishing and the Pandemic', which was published between 2020 and 2022 and includes over two hundred articles featuring a range of voices across Indian publishing.[20] I use the data within this series to locate the place of the brick-and-mortar bookstore both spatially and rhetorically, arguing that this dataset highlights the marginalisation of brick-and-mortar bookstores within the wider context of trade publishing; more importantly, it also reveals a gradual change in this marginalisation as a consequence of the pandemic. Section 4 then considers the changing position of the brick-and-mortar bookstore from another perspective, using a set of case studies to highlight how booksellers actively altered the logic of the field during the pandemic by using social media and digital platforms to perform what Laura Miller calls 'independent bookseller activism'.[21] Finally, Section 5 explores the results of these transformations in 2021 and beyond, focusing on key characteristics that define the logic of the revitalised bookselling field: an expanded network of brick-and-mortar bookstores; the potential for an increase in bibliodiversity; and the changing corporate and conglomerate priorities that have helped to support this renaissance.

1.1 The Logic of the Field

In 1987, the first large-format bookstore in the country, Landmark, opened in Chennai, south India, 'transform[ing] organised book retail' in the country.[22] In the 1990s, Landmark was a partner in the creation of Westland – a distribution company which imported English books into India and soon became the leading book distributor in the country.[23] By 2005, Landmark was a successful chain with multiple outlets across the country, and was (perhaps

---

[20] See 'Publishing and the Pandemic', *Scroll*.

[21] Laura Miller, *Reluctant Capitalists: Bookselling and the Culture of Consumption* (Chicago: University of Chicago Press, 2006).

[22] Bhaskar Bhatt, 'First person: How a publishing executive started helping migrant labourers during the lockdown', *Scroll*, 21 June 2020.

[23] Vinutha Mallya, 'Amazon's Westland plan: Game-changing or gaming the book industry?', *Leftword*, 1 February 2022.

The Brick-and-Mortar Bookstore in Contemporary India   7

inevitably) bought over by India's largest conglomerate, the Tata group; Westland was acquired alongside.[24] Under the Tata group, Landmark continued to expand, while Westland pivoted from distribution to publishing, launching a set of imprints.[25] A little over a decade later, Westland would change hands once again: 'to test interest in India's books market', Amazon acquired first a partial stake, and then complete ownership in 2016.[26] By 2016, the era of Amazon had eclipsed that of the chain, and though Landmark continued to exist, its heyday was over. However, its influence in the book retail landscape had spread – over the years, former Landmark employees had gone on to launch other bookstores, including Odyssey, Fountainhead, and Crossword, currently India's largest bookstore chain.[27] Meanwhile, Westland would continue as a successful publishing house until February 2022, when Amazon announced that it would be shuttering the company overnight.[28]

As a portrait of one bookstore and its legacy – a history cobbled together from newspaper articles, obituaries, blogs, and interviews – the story of Landmark is also a story of the wider context of trade publishing in the 2000s and 2010s: an industry shaped by patterns of import and distribution, retail expansion, local publishing, and conglomerate and corporate takeovers. In other words, a focus on a single bookstore such as Landmark can serve to illuminate what Thompson terms 'the logic of the field', building on Pierre Bourdieu's notion of the field of cultural production to define the publishing industry as a space of plurality and relationality, dependent for its existence on access to, and traffic in, economic, symbolic, and social capital.[29] In his examination of anglophone (largely American and British)

---

[24] Vangmayi Parakala, 'Westland's Gautam Padmanabhan: The comeback man', *Mint*, 28 July 2023.

[25] Ibid.

[26] Mallya, 'Amazon's Westland plan'.

[27] Selina Sheth, 'Walden, Hyderabad (1990–2020): The bookshop that, sadly, could not survive the pandemic', *Scroll*, 6 December 2020.

[28] Mallya, 'Amazon's Westland plan'.

[29] Thompson, *Merchants of Culture*, 5; Pierre Bourdieu, 'The field of cultural production', in *The Book History Reader*, eds. David Finkelstein and Alistair McCleery, 2nd ed. (London: Routledge, 2006), 99–120.

trade publishing, Thompson identifies the logic of the field – the 'set of factors that determine the conditions under which individual agents and organizations can participate in the field'[30] – as defined by changes to the landscape of book retail; the growing influence of literary agents; and conglomeration within publishing corporations.[31] Although Thompson takes the publishing firm as his central focus, his mapping of the field of trade publishing is equally useful to an analysis of any agent or organisation involved in 'the production, sale and distribution of this particular cultural commodity, the book'.[32] The brick-and-mortar bookstore is self-evidently crucial in what Thompson terms the supply and value chains within trade publishing.[33] However, its position in the field is more complex; and the visibility, infrastructure, and value afforded to the bookstore – especially by those within the field – have implications for the overall landscape of book retail and publishing.

Bourdieu's conception of the field has long been useful to scholars of book and publishing history interested in tracing the hierarchies and flows of symbolic and material value in a creative industry. For the purpose of this Element, however, I find working with Thompson's framework particularly useful, both in identifying patterns of events and structural conditions which define the world of trade publishing and undergird the flows of capital within the industry, as well as in tracing these developments chronologically to note larger shifts within the field. Thompson suggests that the workings of the industry are particularly difficult to define, and often unclear even to those within it, likening the processes to 'the grammar of a language: individuals know how to speak correctly ... but they may not be able to formulate these rules in an explicit fashion'.[34] My own interest in bookselling is influenced by my professional experience working in trade publishing in India between 2017 and 2021, and my first-hand observations of the complex, fragmented, and idiosyncratic bookselling landscape. Perceiving the logic of the field from within was, in my experience, identical to Thompson's metaphor of an unspoken grammar. In this Element, therefore, I attempt what Thompson describes as the work of 'an analyst of the

---

[30] Thompson, *Merchants of Culture*, 11. [31] Ibid., 22. [32] Ibid. [33] Ibid., 16.
[34] Ibid., 11.

world of publishing':[35] to view the field from an academic standpoint, and 'discern some order in the plethora of details'[36] by identifying some of the factors and dynamics – the logics of the field – that characterise brick-and-mortar bookselling in the country.

While my analysis follows Thompson's mapping of the field, I refer to it as the 'bookselling field' in order to centre the focus of my analysis. As well, although the field encompasses a range of players and functions, I focus most closely on the relationship of the brick-and-mortar bookstore to two key entities: publishers and distributors, who form its two closest 'links' on the publishing chain. My analysis adopts a qualitative, mixed methods approach that, as Rachel Noorda and Stevie Marsden note, is common to twenty-first-century book studies, especially in explorations of the 'economics of the book trade'.[37] In the absence of comprehensive scholarship on Indian bookselling, this Element draw upon a range of primary sources, including trade publications as well as newspapers and digital news sites, as well as primary data in the form of booksellers' posts on digital platforms, including Instagram, Twitter (now X), and bookstore websites. These different sets of information together offer a glimpse into the workings of the contemporary bookselling field and its transformation over the course of the pandemic.

---

[35] Ibid., 12. [36] Ibid., 14.
[37] Rachel Noorda and Stevie Marsden, 'Twenty-first century book studies: The state of the discipline', *Book History* 22, no. 1 (2019): 385.

2 Brick-and-Mortar Bookselling in Contemporary India

Speaking of anglophone trade publishing in India, Richard Charkin remarks that '[e]verything about India is peculiar as is everything about every book market peculiar'.[38] While the specificities of publishing and bookselling in other anglophone markets have been more extensively discussed, the book market in India can appear even more like Thompson's metaphor of the grammar of a language: its workings intelligible to those within the field, but not necessarily explicit to others. This section explores some key developments in trade bookselling in India, beginning with a brief overview of the anglophone book trade in the country before focusing specifically on contemporary brick-and-mortar bookselling and its relationship to the twin threats of Amazon and the COVID-19 pandemic. I suggest that the uncertain, fragmented bookselling landscape and the economics of trade bookselling work together to define the logic of the field during this time, and serve to place the brick-and-mortar bookstore in a disadvantaged, precarious position even before the onset of the pandemic.

A very brief history of anglophone trade bookselling in India might begin in the 1800s, when Thomas Abraham argues that the 'emergence of "trade" books' in the country can be traced to the establishment of two bookstores: Higginbothams, founded in Madras (now Chennai) in south India in 1844, and Wheeler's, a chain of railway bookshops that was formed around 1877.[39] Successive decades saw the founding of more bookstores and chains, such as the Oxford Book and Stationery Company in 1920; alongside this, the first trade associations within publishing and bookselling were formed, such as among booksellers at the College Street 'book mart' in Calcutta (now Kolkata).[40] A second phase of organisation began post-independence, with a 'sea change in both the publishing and bookselling

---

[38] Richard Charkin, 'Innovation, creativity and the unrealized potential of Indian trade publishing', *Logos* 33, no. 2–3 (December 2022): 52.

[39] Thomas Abraham, 'After midnight: The English trade publishing scene', *Logos* 33, no. 2–3 (December 2022): 30.

[40] Abhijit Gupta, 'The history of the book in the Indian subcontinent', in *The Book: A Global History*, eds. Michael F. Suarez and H. R. Woudhuysen. 1st ed. (Oxford: Oxford University Press, 2013), 569.

situations', as more Indians, writing in English, began to seek publishers within the country.[41] By the 1970s, established and newer publishing firms, such as Oxford University Press, began to set up in Delhi, which became 'the main distribution and publishing centre of the country'.[42] As previously mentioned, 1987 was a watershed moment, with the opening of the first large-format bookstore, Landmark; in the same year, Penguin India began local operations in the country.[43]

Importantly, in these initial decades, Indian laws dictated that international companies could 'only set up as a joint venture with a minority stake'; as a result, partnerships and collaborations were the norm: HarperCollins India, for example, partnered first with local publishing house Rupa and then with the India Today media group.[44] From the perspective of the anglophone book trade, the loosening of these restrictions was a major development of the early 2000s, allowing the 'big six' publishers to establish a more prominent local presence.[45] As a result, the key players in global anglophone trade publishing all entered the field, along with educational and academic publishers such as Dorling Kindersley and Hay House; at the same time, the large-format and chain bookstores expanded and flourished.[46] Then, in 2007, a new era of bookselling began, with the establishment of the online retailer Flipkart, 'India's first online giant', followed by the entry of Amazon India in 2013.[47] This was, perhaps, the most disruptive influence on Indian publishing in decades, and its effects were almost immediately seen in the widespread 'death of the bookstore', as will be discussed later.

It is worth noting that the broad-strokes nature of this history of bookselling in India is significant, not just for what it tells us, but for the gaps in knowledge that it exposes. Scholarly discussions of publishing

---

[41] Abraham, 'After midnight', 32. [42] Ibid., 33. [43] Ibid. [44] Ibid., 34.

[45] The 'big six' refers to the publishing corporations which traditionally dominate anglophone trade publishing: Penguin, Random House, Macmillan, HarperCollins, Simon & Schuster, and Hachette Book Group (see Thompson, *Merchants of Culture*, Appendix 1). The nomenclature has changed over time with further conglomeration, such as the merger of Penguin Random House, which reduced these players to the 'big five'.

[46] Abraham, 'After midnight', 35. [47] Ibid.

history do offer some insight into bookselling, pointing to key patterns in retail expansion, the establishment of international and conglomerate publishing in India and its impact on the anglophone market, and the centralisation of the (book) publishing industry in New Delhi. In incorporating these details of brick-and-mortar bookselling within larger histories of trade publishing, however, these discussions are often brief; and much has happened in the intervening decades which remains, to a large extent, uninvestigated. As Corinna Norrick-Rühl points out, bookselling research is also complicated by the lack of formal archives from which to draw upon, making it harder to fill in these gaps.[48] While acknowledging these gaps in historical context, I turn to a more contemporary time period, exploring some of the factors that characterise brick-and-mortar bookselling across the 2010s and 2020s.

2.1 The Logics of Brick-and-Mortar Bookselling

The threat posed to the brick-and-mortar bookstore by Amazon is a familiar story, but the way this story unfolds is influenced by the specific logics of the bookselling field in each market. In India, I suggest, contemporary brick-and-mortar bookselling is influenced by three factors: the relatively marginal place of trade publishing and bookselling; the fragmentation and uncertainty of brick-and-mortar bookselling; and the price-sensitive book market. These factors work together to characterise the bookselling field as a space of vulnerability and precariousness; in addition, they help to explain Amazon's rapid near-monopoly and the period of the 'death of the bookstore'.

To begin with, as Thompson notes, the world of publishing is made up of a 'plurality of fields'[49]: with trade (general-interest fiction and non-fiction), academic, and educational publishing all defined by, and operating with, different processes. In India, the overall landscape features the added complexity of around 1,500 spoken languages, making English-language publishing a subset within a much larger context.[50] It is important to note

---

[48] Corinna Norrick-Rühl, *Book Clubs and Book Commerce* (Cambridge: Cambridge University Press, 2019), 8.

[49] Thompson, *Merchants of Culture*, 4.

[50] Gupta, 'The history of the book', 553.

that – perhaps unusually, when compared to other markets – trade books form a minuscule segment of the overall book market in India. In terms of numbers, India is a massive market: in 2022, Nielsen reported that 'India is ranked as the third-largest market in the world for print books and is the world's second-biggest Englishspeaking [sic] economy', pointing to its exceptionally young population and rising literacy rates.[51] English-language books make up a considerable proportion of these sales; however, the market is overwhelmingly dominated by academic, rather than trade, publishing; in 2022, for instance, sales of trade books contributed to a mere 3.7% of India's publishing revenue, with the remaining 93.3% coming from educational publishing.[52] Thus, although the absolute numbers make India appear to be one of the world's most attractive book markets, and anglophone trade publishing in the country is represented by both international conglomerates as well as local firms, the actual place of trade publishing is fractional; Charkin describes India as 'a relative minnow on the international stage'.[53]

Naturally, this has had consequences for bookselling. In 2015, Nielsen estimated that there were about 21,000 book retailers in India, of which only 1800 – about 8.5% – were identified as 'trade outlets'; the rest sold solely educational books.[54] In other words, just as anglophone trade *publishing* occupies a relatively minor position within the overall book market – at least in terms of numbers – so too does the anglophone trade *bookstore*. For publishers, these challenges are arguably mitigated by conglomeration, organisation, and economies of scale. While the chain bookstore might share some of these advantages, the stand-alone bookstore does not; trade brick-and-mortar bookstores thus find themselves in a relatively

---

[51] Vikrant Mathur, 'Frankfurt Book Fair 2022: India's book market booms', *Publishers Weekly*, 21 October 2022.

[52] World Intellectual Property Organization, *The Global Publishing Industry in 2022* (Geneva: WIPO, 2023), 6–8. Book markets in the Netherlands and Türkiye follow a similar pattern.

[53] Charkin, 'Innovation, creativity', 53.

[54] Vinutha Mallya, 'Nielsen values Indian publishing at $3.9 Billion', *Publishing Perspectives*, 21 October 2015.

marginalised position within the publishing landscape, simply by virtue of the overall makeup of the book market. This vulnerability is compounded by the fragmentation and uncertainty involved in brick-and-mortar bookselling, perhaps best exemplified by the logistics of the publishing supply chain, which scholarly and industry reports concur is one of the main challenges in the Indian market. As previously mentioned, trade publishers are concentrated in the Delhi-NCR area; this is also true of printing presses.[55] In India, as in other book markets, books move from the presses to distributors, who then supply stock to book retailers. Given the size of the country, this means that the first crucial steps of the supply chain – from publisher to printer to warehouse to retailer – require multiple stakeholders, layers of logistics, and significant time. This staggered process involves multiple 'logistical problems such as warehousing, transportation, inventory, recovery of dues from bookstores and bookstore locations that are difficult to access'.[56] As a result, distribution is unevenly efficient, with more problems faced by non-urban centres and smaller towns 'where the distribution value chain is highly fragmented and requires substantial lead-time before books reach the end user'.[57] As a result, booksellers have observed that the biggest distributors tend to concentrate on sourcing from large publishers, making it more difficult for bookstores to acquire books from smaller or independent presses.[58] The long payment cycles

[55] The territory of 'Delhi-NCR' includes the city of New Delhi as well as the broader 'National Capital Region' (NCR) which covers districts in neighbouring states; notably Haryana and Uttar Pradesh, where many trade publishers' offices are located. See 'National Capital Region Planning Board'. The two largest presses for trade publishing are both located in the Delhi-NCR; see 'About Us', ThomsonPress; 'Company Profile', ReplikaPress.

[56] Kanishka Gupta, 'How does the life of a book change as it goes from publisher to bookseller?' *Scroll*, 9 December 2017.

[57] Association of Publishers of India and EY-Parthenon, *Value Proposition of the India Publishing: Trends, Challenges, and the Future of the Industry | May 2021* (Ernst & Young, 2021), 25.

[58] Padmini Ray Murray, Rashmi Dhanwani, and Kavya Iyer Ramalingam, *India Literature and Publishing Sector Study | December 2020 – May 2021* (British Council, 2021), 24.

created by this extended chain, combined with the idiosyncratic 'sale-on-return' policy which continues to be followed in bookselling worldwide, make the economics of bookselling tricky and uncertain, and can even cause publishers to choose not to supply books to certain bookstores in response to frequent delays in payment.[59] As a result, to varying degrees, all brick-and-mortar bookstores face challenges in predicting, coordinating, and maintaining a supply of books.

These issues of prediction and coordination form another major challenge in the Indian book market, which is beset by a notorious lack of data, not only in scholarly discussion, but also within the industry itself; as Thomas Abraham – currently managing director of Hachette India – notes, '[t]here is alas no reliable data whatsoever for trade market sizes from 1947 or even ... recent decades'.[60] While the World Intellectual Property Organization report for 2022 states that Nielsen BookScan, the industry standard for sales data, covers 'a significant part of the organized market', Abraham estimates the numbers at 'about 50–65 per cent of the market depending on the type of book', and suggests using an 'extrapolation multiplier of about 1.5x' for more accurate data on book sales.[61] Trade publishing also lacks the institutional frameworks that are present in an educational or academic context; these books are not ordered by educational institutions or prescribed on syllabi. Practically speaking, this means that a significant amount of expenditure and labour is involved in tracking bookstore sales; in the absence of online data, distributors and publishers rely on informal communication between their sales representatives and booksellers in order to gain data on stock and sales.[62] Bookseller Subodh Sankar points out that this activity, too, is limited to metropolitan cities; elsewhere, publishers tend to track the number of copies sold *to* distributors, rather than those sold *by* bookstores, and thus have 'zero visibility about

---

[59] Gupta, 'How does the life of a book change'; for a discussion of the 'sale on return' policy in publishing, see for instance Thomas, 'Bookselling', 403.

[60] Abraham, 'After midnight', 35.

[61] WIPO, *The Global Publishing Industry in 2022*, 31; Abraham, 'After midnight', 35. In my time working in trade publishing in India, we used a similar multiplier to estimate sales.

[62] Gupta, 'How does the life of a book change'.

secondary sales' – that is, actual sales to customers.[63] With no organised data on bookstore sales, the exact number of functioning bookstores in the country is equally uncertain. This results in a vicious cycle for bookselling: the degree of this historic lack of data is its own deterrent against the industry investing more money or labour in producing this data; and as a result, the book market remains disorganised and fragmented. Anish Chandy, a publishing professional, argues that the problem is systemic: 'the underlying model of selling books offline is shaky'.[64] Any effort to combat these challenges would, therefore, require considerable investment in transforming an entire industry.

This investment might not be immediately forthcoming for a number of reasons. Questions of money are always a concern in trade bookselling; in India, this is compounded not just by its minor place within the larger publishing industry and the fragmentation of its supply chain, but also by the extraordinary price-sensitivity of the market. In fact, 'one of the most distinctive aspects of the vast market in India [is] a traditionally low price point'.[65] A Nielsen survey conducted in 2020 saw respondents estimate their preferred retail price for a paperback at between 200 to 400 rupees (that is, roughly, between £2 and £4).[66] Abraham similarly estimates that a paperback priced at £9.99 in the UK would retail in India for around £4.[67] At the same time, publishers' costs have only continued to grow, with sharp increases in the price of paper, fuel, and freight over the last decades.[68] While India does not have a system enforcing a fixed price for books, it does enforce a 'maximum retail price' or MRP, which must be printed on commodities including books; this prevents retailers from charging more than the printed price.[69] For trade

[63] Subodh Sankar, 'What the pandemic means for this independent bookstore which thrives on its physical space', *Scroll*, 22 August 2020.
[64] Gupta, 'How does the life of a book change'.
[65] Porter Anderson, 'Coronavirus impact: Nielsen book India on readers in the pandemic', *Publishing Perspectives*, 15 July 2020.
[66] Ibid.
[67] Abraham, 'After midnight', 36.
[68] Association of Publishers of India and EY-Parthenon, *Value Proposition of the India Publishing*, 27.
[69] Anupam Manur, 'Time to abolish the MRP', *The Hindu*, 22 July 2015.

publishing, which already forms such a small component of the total book market, the possibility of raising prices is slim, and publishers often choose to incur lower margins or even losses instead.[70] On their part, brick-and-mortar booksellers face other rising costs, such as rent, and have no power to adjust book prices in response; as Anish Chandy notes, '[t]he offline retailer is the most vulnerable entity in this cycle'.[71] Taken together, then, the field of English-language trade bookselling in India is characterised by a fractional market share; a fragmented landscape with no infrastructure in place to record either book retailers or book sales; a system of warehousing and distribution which poses both monetary and logistical inefficiencies; and a highly price-sensitive readership.

These factors – present in the earliest forms of organised bookselling in India – continue to shape the industry in the present day. However, from the 2010s onwards, the field was dramatically altered by the introduction of an alternative to the uncertainty, disorganisation, and economic constraints of physical bookselling, with the introduction of a retail system that could promise instant data, effortless logistics, and high discounts. The next section explores the ways in which Amazon's arrival in the Indian context quickly led to a monopoly of online retail, exacerbating the challenges faced by brick-and-mortar bookstores.

2.2 The Brick-and-Mortar Bookstore in the Age of Amazon

In *The Late Age of Print*, Ted Striphas suggests that '[r]ather than referring to Amazon.com as an online or Internet bookseller, perhaps it would be more apt to call it a large-scale, direct-to-consumer warehouse bookseller', a perspective he sees as essential in placing 'warehouses or order-fulfilment facilities center stage, where they belong'.[72] This statement is perhaps especially relevant in the Indian context, where the origin story of Amazon is linked most strongly to its warehousing and logistical efficiencies. When setting up Amazon in the United States, Jeff Bezos famously made the

---

[70] Porter Anderson, 'Frankfurt week: A new report on the Indian book market', *Publishing Perspectives*, 17 October 2022.

[71] Gupta, 'How does the life of a book change'.

[72] Striphas, *The Late Age*, 101.

decision to focus on books precisely because of their systems of organisation, such as the internationally adopted ISBN code and inventory processes.[73] However, as the previous section has demonstrated, these systems barely existed in the Indian context; bookselling and publishing continued to lack infrastructure or data processes even as of 2013. In addition, the India of 2013 was a cash economy; its citizens were far from digitally native, with barely 30% of Indians possessing an internet connection; and, most significantly, governmental policies prevented 'foreign multibrand retailers from selling directly to consumers online'.[74] Thus, when Amazon arrived in India, it did so in the guise of a third-party aggregator rather than a bookstore. In an article announcing its launch, the *BBC* described its operations as follows: '[s]ellers send their goods to Amazon's warehouse near Mumbai. When an order is placed, Amazon packs and sends the order to the customer'.[75] In a similar vein, the country manager of Amazon India declared that their initial vision was 'to become a trusted and meaningful sales channel for retailers of all sizes across India'.[76] Striphas's observation that Amazon is a warehouse, and not a bookseller, is thus true in its most literal sense in the Indian context.

Importantly, Amazon also adjusted its business model in other ways, adapting to the aforementioned idiosyncrasies of the Indian market. In the initial years, Amazon introduced cash-on-delivery payment options, a first for the company; in addition, they offered a version of the app that was compatible with lower internet speeds, and expanded to other local languages.[77] Perhaps most conveniently, though, Amazon's positioning as a 'marketplace' meant that the company could insist that pricing decisions were out of its control – this was ostensibly left up to the individual retailers, or 'sellers', as Amazon termed them. The result of these decisions was inevitable. Amazon India might have had to follow a different playbook

---

[73] Ibid., 102.

[74] Vijay Govindarajan and Anita Warren, 'How Amazon adapted its business model to India', *Harvard Business Review*, 20 July 2016.

[75] 'Amazon launches first online shopping site in India', *BBC*, 5 June 2013.

[76] Ibid.

[77] Danny D'Cruze, 'India's unique e-commerce story: Insights from Amazon India's VP on the last 10 years', *Business Today*, 6 June, 2023.

from other territories, but its impact on book retail, at least, was ultimately familiar; by 2015, just two years after its entry into the market, 50% of English-language trade bookselling was taking place online.[78]

Given that brick-and-mortar bookselling was beset by a lack of data and organisation, it is perhaps unsurprising that the publishing industry saw benefits in the Amazon model. By virtue of its logistical reach – and its ability to offer discounts that bookstores could not match – Amazon could serve more readers than the country's entire physical bookselling ecosystem could manage. Recognising the historical problems with warehousing and distribution, Amazon had focused on expansion of storage space from its earliest days. By 2015, they were able to deliver to almost every pincode in the country.[79] By 2021, the company had 'more than 60 fulfilment centers . . . offering 43 million cubic feet to its sellers'.[80] The disorganised network of brick-and-mortar bookstores in the country could not possibly make such promises; nor did they have marketing budgets to compare with Amazon and Flipkart, who could run front-page advertisements advertising their exclusive deals for bestsellers.[81] As publishers prioritised Amazon, the effects were seen across the field. For example, distributors saw disruptions in their business as publishers chose to deal directly with Amazon retailers; this meant that online 'sellers' would now buy books directly from the publisher, and their stock would be managed by Amazon's fulfilment centres rather than distributor warehouses, as was the norm for brick-and-mortar bookselling.[82] From the point of view of the consumer, the value of Amazon – convenience, affordability, range, access – was self-evident. While Amazon could maintain that it had no control over the deep discounting on its site, there was no doubt that these discounts were present, and heavily advertised, across the platform, which was 'willing to take a loss on each transaction in order to grow its customer base'.[83] Alongside lowered prices, Amazon could also offer a wider range of titles; not just because they faced no constraints in physical shelf space, but also because they could

---

[78] Chandrasekaran, 'The death of the bookstore'. [79] Ibid.
[80] Amazon Staff, 'Amazon India strengthens its fulfilment and delivery network', Amazon India, 1 October 2021.
[81] John, 'Why bookshops are closing'.
[82] D'Cruze, 'India's unique e-commerce story'. [83] Ibid.

more easily import titles from the UK or the United States, 'as they [received] enough orders to make the air freight economical'.[84] Consequently, the years between 2013 and 2020 saw a series of transformations in the brick-and-mortar bookselling landscape. Thomas Abraham vividly summarises the consequences of 'deeper discounts and the scorched-earth policy' of e-retailers on brick-and-mortar bookselling from 2013 onwards:

> most of the chains died within the decade and what we have now is effectively one major chain (Crossword) and a series of regional multi-outlet stores (Landmark, Starmark, Om, Sapna). Alongside the chains, the churn of the 2010s saw over one hundred stores shut down including some iconic indie stores ... with online (read maybe Amazon) growing exponentially.[85]

Abraham is oddly hesitant to point to the influence of Amazon as a certainty; however, it is undeniable that the meteoric ascent of Amazon went hand-in-hand with the 'death of the bookstore'; as bookstores across the country continued to close, online retail could only move closer to monopoly. Amazon had quickly grown to become a key player in the field, and its presence as the largest, most powerful bookstore in the country seemed impossible to deny, challenge, or escape. Then, in 2020, the onset of the COVID-19 pandemic introduced a new set of variables which would crucially alter some of these logics.

2.3 The Brick-and-Mortar Bookstore and the COVID-19 Pandemic

The COVID-19 pandemic had both immediate and long-lasting effects on the retail and creative sectors worldwide. In India, pandemic measures were both swift and harsh, taking the form of a complex series of extensive lockdowns. The first nationwide lockdown, 'Lockdown 1.0', lasted from

---

[84] Saumya Ancheri, 'Why Mumbai's iconic Strand Book Stall is shutting', *Condé Nast Traveller India*, 22 February 2018.

[85] Abraham, 'After midnight', 35.

25 March to 14 April 2020; this was subsequently extended in three further phases, lasting until 31 May 2020. During the first two lockdowns, there was a complete prohibition of all industry, commercial activity, or transit, with the exception of what would come to be called 'essential services': food, banking, telecommunication, and utilities, among others.[86] Significantly, 'e-commerce delivery services' faced similar restrictions, and were only allowed to sell a limited set of goods on their platforms during this time.[87] This stands in contrast to other book markets, where sites like Amazon could continue to sell all products; as Claire Squires observes, in territories such as the UK 'there really was no threat at all to ... access to books online' during the pandemic.[88]

Later phases of lockdowns in May added a new layer of complexity, as individual states were divided into 'containment zones', classified as red, orange, and green zones based on the number of infections in the neighbourhood.[89] Malls and shopping centres remained closed across all zones, but 'standalone (single) shops, neighbourhood (colony) shops and shops in residential complexes ... in urban areas' were now permitted to open in lower-risk areas, 'without any distinction of essential and non-essential'; however, e-commerce was still restricted to 'essential goods'.[90] Transport was similarly complex. In red zones, '[m]ovement of individuals and vehicles' was restricted to 'permitted activities'; orange zones allowed '[i]nter-district movement' for 'permitted activities'; and green zones permitted 'inter-state movement of goods' without restriction.[91] Finally, from 8 June 2020 onwards, a three-phase 'Unlock' was announced, with the gradual lessening of all restrictions. A night-time curfew remained in effect,

---

[86] Winter M. Thayer, Md Zabir Hasan, Prithvi Sankhla, and Shivam Gupta, 'An interrupted time series analysis of the lockdown policies in India: A national-level analysis of COVID-19 incidence', *Health Policy and Planning* 36, no. 5 (June 3, 2021): 622.

[87] Ibid.

[88] Squires, 'Essential? Different? Exceptional?'

[89] 'MHA Order and Guidelines Dated 1.5.2020 about Extension of Lock Down beyond 4.5.2020', Government of India Ministry of Home Affairs, 1 May 2020.

[90] Ibid. [91] Ibid.

but at all other times there was 'no restriction on inter-State and intra-State movement of persons and goods'.[92]

These restrictions had a profound and unexpected effect on the book trade, as the logistical complexities that previously challenged brick-and-mortar bookselling began to work, somewhat ironically, in its favour. The initial strict lockdowns naturally adversely affected the brick-and-mortar bookstore; but, unlike markets like the UK, where books were still just a click away, in India the 'essential services' mandate was extended to online retail. As restrictions began to ease, stand-alone shops – which included many bookstores across the country – were allowed to operate within their neighbourhood 'zones', while e-commerce continued to be restricted to essential services. Even as these restrictions on online retail were lifted, the logistics of the supply chain began to come into play. If warehouses were located in containment zones, no movement was possible; furthermore, inter-district and inter-state travel was complicated, requiring permits, and subject to change on short notice if states or districts saw an uptick in infection, which would mean that they were 're-zoned'. Then there was the question of labour. Public transport for private citizens was still banned, which meant that warehouse workers and truck operators – many of whom, as migrant workers, had returned to their hometowns – had no way of reporting to work.[93] Consequently, once Amazon was allowed to make deliveries, whether essential or non-essential, its logistical advantages no longer existed. The size of the country also meant that policies issued by the centre were not necessarily followed by individual states, with reports throughout all phases of trucks being detained by the police or local authorities.[94] In addition, India would continue to tighten measures as

---

[92] 'MHA Order Dt. 30.5.2020 with Guidelines on Extension of LD in Containment Zones and Phased Reopening', Government of India Ministry of Home Affairs, 30 May 2020.

[93] Shweta Punj, Anilesh S Mahajan, M. G. Arun, and Kiran Tare, 'Meeting the demand for supply', *India Today*, 13 April 2020.

[94] 'Covid-19 lockdown: Government says no ban on inter-state movement of trucks', *India Today*, 13 April 2020.

infection rates periodically surged, as with the particularly harsh second wave in early 2021.[95]

It is not unusual that COVID-19 disrupted retail supply chains; but it *is* significant that its occurrence in India led to a situation in which, at least for a brief period of time, the brick-and-mortar bookstore was at a comparative advantage to the e-commerce giant. As stand-alone stores were allowed to open, bookstore workers could go in to work, and had access to some stock, however limited: the books on their shelves. This advantage did not last long; and it occurred during an uncertain, challenging, inopportune moment. Nevertheless, I argue that this was a key factor which would go on to transform the logic of the field of contemporary brick-and-mortar bookselling.

---

[95] 'India coronavirus: New record deaths as virus engulfs India', *BBC*, 2 May 2021.

3 Bookselling and the Pandemic: A Transformation in the Field

On 21 March 2020, three days before India's first national lockdown was announced, the Indian news website *Scroll* published an article titled 'Could the coronavirus pandemic lock down Indian publishing for some time?'[96] Between March 2020 and June 2021, *Scroll* would publish a total of 231 related articles in a series called 'Publishing and the Pandemic'. Curated by literary agent Kanishka Gupta, it aimed to be a 'comprehensive series of reports, commentaries, and first-person accounts of the impact of the Pandemic on publishing in the Indian subcontinent'.[97] The series is, undoubtedly, comprehensive, featuring the voices of nearly every agent involved in the industry; as well, despite the ostensible focus on the pandemic, many of the articles discuss developments across the last decade of publishing. As such, it is a valuable single dataset on the state of contemporary publishing in India, including brick-and-mortar bookselling. Evaluating where and how bookselling is discussed within this extensive series can offer – however partial or incomplete – a snapshot of the bookselling landscape as of 2020, as well as insight into how brick-and-mortar bookselling is perceived and valued by the wider publishing industry. This section focuses on articles within the 'Publishing and the Pandemic' series in order to construct an understanding of the state of bookselling in the years immediately leading up to and including the pandemic. I suggest that, taken as a whole, the series reveals a set of interconnected factors which define the place of the brick-and-mortar bookstore across 2020 and 2021: a scattered, disorganised bookselling landscape, with brick-and-mortar bookstores facing systemic and logistical challenges pre-dating the pandemic; the marginalisation of brick-and-mortar bookselling within the wider publishing field; and, crucially, the beginnings of a transformation in the field.

---

[96] Kanishka Gupta, 'Could the coronavirus pandemic lock down Indian publishing for some time?' *Scroll*, 21 March 2020.

[97] 'Kanishka Gupta', *Publishers Marketplace*.

3.1 Publishing, the Pandemic, and the Bookselling Landscape

Soon after the first article in 'Publishing and the Pandemic' was published, the series began to grow quickly, with articles published regularly across 2020 and 2021; at its peak, an average of twenty articles per month were published between May and December 2020. The series curator, Kanishka Gupta, is an important figure in Indian trade publishing, as a leading literary agent whose authors have won prestigious literary awards; in 2020, an author he represents was shortlisted for the Booker Prize.[110] Perhaps as a result of Gupta's own place within the industry, the series is notably representative in reach and breadth, and addresses an impressive range of subjects. Interestingly, these articles are also made available to a wide audience: *Scroll* is a news website with a general readership, rather than an industry-facing publication, and while there are no recent statistics on readership, in 2016 the website received almost four million unique visits per month.[111]

The articles across the series can broadly be grouped into the following categories, based on the primary focus of each piece (see Table 1). As might be expected, the largest proportion of articles discuss the wider impact of COVID-19 on the entire industry. This is a wide-ranging category, with articles focusing on a range of specific organisations and individuals, including book reviewers, literary agents, freelance workers, women in publishing, printing presses, and book cover designers, among others. Several articles focus on community libraries and archives as well as consecratory institutions such as literary prizes and festivals, and a significant proportion consist of personal essays by writers, excerpts from published fiction and non-fiction, and general discussions of books and literature, such as articles on how the pandemic might affect genre trends.

A relatively small number of articles consider readership, looking specifically at book clubs in different Indian cities; and a sombre collection pays tribute to the memory of publishing figures who lost their lives in the pandemic. As the series focuses on the larger context of publishing in the subcontinent, there are also a number of articles discussing publishing in local languages as well as in countries outside of India, most prominently

Table 1 Categories featured within 'Publishing and the Pandemic'

Category	Number of articles
Industry: Impact of COVID−19	33
Offline bookselling[98]	34
Personal essays	29
Publishing in the subcontinent/overseas	19
Creative fiction and nonfiction	19
Libraries and archives	18
Publishing firms	18
Indian-language publishing	17
Books/literature	16
Literary festivals, awards, residencies	16
Obituaries	7
Book clubs	5

Pakistan and Bangladesh.[99] Most significantly, from the point of view of this Element, physical bookselling appears to be a prime category, making up 15% of all articles within the series; there are no articles that focus specifically on Amazon or e-retail. Going purely by the numbers, it might seem as if bookselling occupies a high-priority spot within the series – and, by extension, plays a vital role in the industry. This prominent presence is logical: retail was the first and hardest-hit sector of the industry; the closure of bookstores affected every step of the publishing chain, from author to reader; and to the series' general readership, the bookstore is perhaps the most familiar element of the world of publishing (outside of the book).

---

[98] I use 'offline', rather than 'brick-and-mortar', as this category also includes articles which focus on informal physical bookselling such as street markets and sales on trains.

[99] Given the focus of this Element, these articles are excluded from all discussion within this section.

However, looking more closely at the content of the articles, a somewhat different picture emerges.

In a September 2020 article in the series, 'Will the pandemic enable us to imagine our cities with more bookstores?', publisher and bookseller Sudhanva Deshpande writes: 'How many bookstores does Delhi have? Sadly, no one knows, and it is hard to even hazard a guess'.[100] Deshpande speaks of a single city – the capital of the country, in which much of the trade publishing industry is concentrated – and yet points out that nobody in the industry can accurately capture its bookselling landscape. The lack of data reinforces the role of this series as an important intervention in making brick-and-mortar bookstores more visible to both the industry and the general public. In some cases, 'Publishing and the Pandemic' is the first major record of certain bookstores; for example, it contains the earliest online mention of Sudarsan Books in Nagercoil, south India.[101] At the same time, though, the series also makes visible the patterns of fragmentation and unevenness present throughout the bookselling landscape of the country.

Although bookselling is the subject of a significant proportion of the series, it is clear from the start that the landscape under discussion is an incomplete one. Accounting for all mentions of English-language bookstores across the series still results in a map in which large sections of the country, particularly in the central and north-western regions, remain completely unaddressed. These gaps in the map persist even when factoring in Crossword outlets across the country (the chain, somewhat surprisingly, is not discussed within the series).[102] Significantly, this unevenness is reinforced

---

[100] Sudhanva Deshpande, 'Will the pandemic enable us to imagine our cities with more bookstores?' *Scroll*, 12 September 2020.

[101] Mythili Sundaram and Ram Sarangan, 'How to open a new bookshop during the pandemic: The story of Sudarsan Books of Nagercoil', *Scroll*, 22 December 2020. The store set up its own website in 2021.

[102] See https://padlet.com/booksellingandthepandemic/bookstorementions for a map of anglophone bookstores mentioned across the series and https://padlet.com/booksellingandthepandemic/crosswordoutlets for a map of Crossword's branches as of 2020.

by first-person accounts throughout the series. Deshpande, for example, describes the situation in Delhi, a city with 'a population as large as that of Bulgaria' where English-language bookstores are concentrated in the central and southern regions, requiring people in other neighbourhoods to travel a considerable distance to access a physical bookstore.[103] In this respect, Delhi is at an advantage; a bookseller from Bhubaneswar, the capital city of the eastern state of Odisha, states that '[m]illions of people in our country have never been inside a bookstore', citing interactions with customers who have only encountered books in classrooms.[104] In other cities, bookstores are anomalies – the town of Mussoorie in north India has only one general bookstore, as does Patna, the capital city of Bihar.[105] Across the country, in the southern state of Tamil Nadu, the town of Nagercoil saw its first trade bookstore open '[a]t the turn of the millennium'.[106] Hyderabad, a metropolitan city with 6.8 million residents, could boast of only one remaining independent bookstore as of 2020.[107] And even a single bookstore is an advantage; the organiser of a book club in Rampur – a city barely 200 kilometres from Delhi – begins her article in the series with the statement, 'There are no bookstores in Rampur.'[108] Among publishing scholars and literacy activists, the phrase 'book desert' is often used to denote neighbourhoods with low average book ownership;[109] the information gained across this series suggests that large sections of India are book*selling* deserts.

---

[103] Deshpande, 'Will the pandemic enable us to imagine our cities with more bookstores?'

[104] Satabdi Misra, 'How did a travelling indie bookshop close down and then re-open in the middle of a pandemic?', *Scroll*, 25 November 2020.

[105] Karan Madhok, 'Will Mussoorie's Cambridge Book Depot open after the pandemic? Residents and visitors are hoping so', *Scroll*, 6 June 2021; Harsh Aditya, 'Nine locations and one pandemic later, this independent bookstore still woos Patna's booklovers', *Scroll*, 6 March 2021.

[106] Sundaram and Sarangan, 'How to open a new bookshop during the pandemic'.

[107] Mallik Thatipalli, 'Low costs, moderate hopes: How Hyderabad's last independent bookstore is trying to survive Covid-19', *Scroll*, 15 October 2020.

[108] Tarana Husain Khan, 'The journey of the Rampur Book Club shows how reading communities responded to the pandemic', *Scroll*, 20 August 2020.

[109] See 'The Book Desert Map', Unite for Literacy.

The omission of Crossword in these discussions is also a reminder that 'Publishing and the Pandemic' is not an empirical dataset, but a curated series; as such, it is worth noting that the makeup of the bookstores that *do* find mention within these articles are overwhelmingly concentrated in urban, metropolitan cities. Table 2 lists the number of times a specific city is mentioned in a discussion of brick-and-mortar bookstores within the series. This table lists the number of times each city is featured, rather than unique mentions of bookstores; thus, while bookstores in Delhi are

Table 2 Cities mentioned in connection with brick-and-mortar bookstores

City, state	Mentions	City, state	Mentions
New Delhi, Delhi	20	Mumbai, Maharashtra	12
Bengaluru, Karnataka	11	Gurgaon, Haryana	6
Chennai, Tamil Nadu	4	Margao, Goa	4
Hyderabad, Telangana	3	Kolkata, West Bengal	3
Pune, Maharashtra	2	Amritsar, Punjab	1
Jaipur, Rajasthan	1	Bareilly, Uttar Pradesh	1
Bhubaneswar, Odisha	1	Noida, Uttar Pradesh	1
Gangtok, Sikkim	1	Kohima, Nagaland	1
Guwahati, Assam	1	Nagercoil, Tamil Nadu	1
Mussoorie, Uttarakhand	1	Panaji, Goa	1
Patna, Bihar	1	Shillong, Meghalaya	1
Srinagar, Jammu and Kashmir	1	Varanasi, Uttar Pradesh	1

mentioned twenty times within the series, a handful of bookstores – three of them sharing the same pincode – receive multiple features. As the table shows, representation within the series is skewed towards major cities such as Delhi, Mumbai, and Bengaluru, reinforcing the fact that some regions of the country receive substantially more attention than others.

This disproportionality also implies other inequalities; for example, it is likely that metropolitan cities *do* have more bookstores, and these are likely to be more better connected in terms of transport, making stock delivery from distributors and visits from publishers' sales representatives easier. These bookstores are also likely to have more capital – economic, social, symbolic – all of which work together to provide, and sustain, their visibility and power, while other bookstores might be neglected or even unknown to members of the industry. Deshpande observes in his article that '[w]e really cannot have cities where populations the size of small nations are not serviced by bookstore',[110] but the series suggests that this appears to be precisely the state of contemporary bookselling in 2020 – with a limited range of bookstores in a limited set of regions commanding the bulk of attention, as well as clear biases that exist within the industry in terms of which bookstores receive attention and visibility. And, even where brick-and-mortar bookstores do exist, their existence is precarious – a fact that is reiterated throughout accounts by booksellers, who list a host of factors affecting their survival that extend before, throughout, and beyond the pandemic.

3.2 'Deeper Cultural and Systemic Problems': Bookselling before the Pandemic

From the first article of the series – which observes that 'once the virus had entered India, orders for books from brick-and-mortar bookshops almost halved'[111] – 'Publishing and the Pandemic' explores many of the factors that affected the book trade, from debating the question of whether books should be classified as 'essential commodities' to the challenge of bookstores having to continue to pay rents and salaries and the impact of lockdowns on

---

[110] Deshpande, 'Will the pandemic enable us to imagine our cities with more bookstores?'

[111] Gupta, 'Could the coronavirus pandemic lock down Indian publishing?'

the logistics of receiving and making deliveries.[112] As lockdowns began to ease, booksellers and publishers worried about whether customers would return to buying books offline, and what 'the new normal' would look like.[113] These discussions are largely similar to those taking place across book markets globally, as several territories dealt with identical issues of 'essential service' mandates, supply chain disruptions, and lowered footfall in retail.[114] At the same time, though, accounts from booksellers across the series also emphasise that many of the challenges they face pre-date the pandemic, with a lack of visibility, organisation, and legal protections contributing to their marginalisation in the field.

In *The Late Age of Print*, Ted Striphas reminds scholars to consider the 'banal circumstances' that might explain bookstore closures, rather than assuming a single villain such as the big-box bookstore – or, from the perspective of this Element, Amazon or the pandemic.[115] Booksellers' accounts within the series are a testament to this reminder: looming largest across these accounts, far larger than the threat of e-commerce or the pandemic, is the question of rent. This affects booksellers across the country, from Full Circle in Delhi's Khan Market – which counts amongst the twenty-five most expensive retail locations in the world[116] – to smaller locations, such as a bookstore in Bhubaneswar whose 'small shack' was destroyed by the authorities, and whose landlord evicted them 'to make way for a

---

[112] See, for instance, Rajni Bahri Malhotra and Anuj Bahri Malhotra, 'What led Delhi's Bahrisons to open a new bookshop in the capital during the pandemic?', *Scroll*, 19 October 2020; Thomas Abraham, 'What can publishers, booksellers (and readers) do for the books business to recover after Covid-19?', *Scroll*, 25 April 2020; Manjari Sahay, 'Independent bookshops: What the lockdown, Covid-19 and its aftermath may mean for them', *Scroll*, 8 May 2020.

[113] Suhit Kelkar, 'What will masks, physical distancing, and public fear of Covid-19 mean for Mumbai's booksellers?', *Scroll*, 11 June 2020.

[114] Squires, 'Essential? Different? Exceptional?'

[115] Striphas, *The Late Age*, 55.

[116] Priyanka Malhotra, 'The pandemic claims an iconic bookshop as Full Circle Bookstore in Delhi's Khan Market closes', *Scroll*, 7 June 2020; 'Delhi's Khan Market World's 22nd Priciest High Street Retail Location', *The Economic Times*, 22 November 2023.

restaurant'.[117] Higher rents are accompanied by regulatory restrictions; for example, Ajay Mago, the owner of a chain of bookstores in malls across north India, points out that these costs are compounded by the maintenance charges levied by malls. Alongside this, stock deliveries cannot be made during the mall's working hours, 'which means an additional cost' involved in supplying his stores.[118] Higher rents can also have a knock-on effect: the owner of a bookstore in Kolkata, Mohan's Bookshop, states that sales were adversely affected when a cinema that used to be located directly opposite the store was forced to close down, drastically affecting footfall; the bookstore closed during the pandemic.[119] Rent is, admittedly, an obvious factor which necessarily affects all physical retail, but it is nevertheless a key 'banal circumstance' that cuts across the bookselling landscape, irrespective of the visibility or social capital that the bookstore might command. As bookstores are also scattered across the country, largely stand-alone and family-run, this leaves them particularly vulnerable to economic precariousness – which would only be exacerbated by the pandemic.

The system of distribution and import, too, is a 'banal circumstance' that adds to the bookstore's vulnerability. Though distribution has long been a challenge in the trade, booksellers' first-person accounts in this series make clearer some of the specific complexities in these processes. Raman Shresta, the owner of Rachna Books in the northern state of Sikkim, outlines his experience of receiving stock:

> [I]n Delhi, books are delivered in half a day. . . . If I were to place an order today, many factors come into play. The books should be available with the distributor in Kolkata. If they are, they will have to be despatched [*sic*] by courier. . . . The courier charge for one book means we will be selling

---

[117] Satabdi Mishra, 'How did a travelling indie bookshop close down and then re-open in the middle of a pandemic?', *Scroll*, 25 November 2020.

[118] Kanishka Gupta, 'How a bookshop-in-mall chain learnt to stop worrying about, and start loving, the new normal', *Scroll*, 30 October 2020.

[119] Rohan Datta, 'How Kolkata's famous Mohan's Bookshop lost its battle against the Covid-19 pandemic', *Scroll*, 2 May 2021.

> the book at a loss. ... If sent by road, a consignment takes two weeks, and that is if there are no blockades and landslides. If the books are not available at the distributors, we have to wait until they arrive from the publishers' warehouses. ... A box of books arriving from Kolkata or Delhi changes three lorries and four warehouses before reaching us on the shoulders of porters. We have to pay for each step of the journey.[120]

Shresta's narration involves multiple factors – availability, time, labour, and political and environmental conditions – each of which involves additional cost. It also reiterates the split that emerges between the relatively advantaged bookstores in well-connected cities, and those more far-flung. The challenges he outlines are likely to be faced by bookstores in other, less-connected regions of the country; in addition, the logistical uncertainty is compounded by higher costs of delivery, further affecting bookstores' ability to match the high discounts of online retailers such as Amazon. Shresta's account is a valuable illustration of the multifaceted infrastructural challenges that continue to shape bookselling and publishing in the country, and bookstores' dependence upon multiple infrastructural conditions that are out of their hands (and, perhaps, beyond the control of the publishing industry as a whole).

To further complicate matters, even where logistical systems are smooth, brick-and-mortar bookstores face another challenge related to distribution. Acquiring English-language books – many of which are published in the United States or UK and imported into India – is a fraught issue. Mahika Chaturvedi and Sonal Narain, booksellers at The Book Shop, New Delhi, point to the problem of 'import rights [conditions] arbitrarily thrust upon brick and mortar stores but not applicable to online sellers'.[121] As they explain, books published by independent presses in the United States or UK can only be ordered by bookstores if they are

---

[120] Kanishka Gupta, 'Six indie bookstores have founded an association of bookshops. What do they hope to achieve?', *Scroll*, 31 May 2020.

[121] Mahika Chaturvedi and Sonal Narain, 'The many ways in which Delhi's The Bookshop reinvented itself during the pandemic', *Scroll*, 13 November 2020.

distributed in India through a 'big five' publisher. Presses who are not distributed in this way, especially American presses such as Dalkey Archive and Carcanet, cannot be directly imported by bookstores, in what they call 'one area where we are still colonized under the commonwealth trade laws'.[122] Re-sellers, however, are free to make these books available on platforms like Amazon.[123] In other words, whether the problem is of logistics of delivery or of import, the brick-and-mortar store faces constraints in supply; and, as the booksellers at The Book Shop observe, in both cases the online retailer stands to benefit.

This last point forms a third challenge echoed by booksellers across the board: the concern that 'there is no policy framework ... to protect independent businesses against the unhinged expansion of e-retailers'.[124] The lack of legal protections makes brick-and-mortar bookstores particularly vulnerable, even in comparison to other sectors of retail, which have more robust trade associations or organised bodies to lobby for their cause. The owner of Wayword and Wise, a bookstore in Mumbai, uses his article to highlight the 'deeper cultural and systemic problems' caused by 'the lack of government support and protection for the book trade'.[125] Throughout the series, booksellers and publishers also call attention to the absence of any regulations governing book pricing, such as the Lang Law followed in France.[126] The disorganised landscape, economic precariousness, and absence of regulatory frameworks is a potent combination – but, in fact, the series points to an even more significant factor that threatens the survival of the brick-and-mortar bookstore: its marginalisation *within* the publishing field.

3.3 'Systemic Lack of Support': Bookselling in the Field

Describing the state of bookselling in November 2020, Anish Chandy remarks, 'bookstores have been suffering for years. The pandemic has

---

[122] Ibid. [123] Ibid. [124] Ibid.

[125] Selina Sheth, 'Mumbai's elegantly curated Wayword & Wise bookshop refuses to go online despite the pandemic. Why?', *Scroll*, 15 November 2020.

[126] See, for example, Abraham, 'What can publishers, booksellers (and readers) do'; Gupta, 'Six indie bookstores'.

become the shove off the cliff.[127] As discussed earlier, Amazon undoubtedly played a pivotal role in this suffering, resulting in a spate of bookstore closures long before the pandemic. Throughout this series, however, what emerges more clearly is the role that others in the field, such as publishers and distributors, have played in the 'age of Amazon'. Most importantly, the series makes visible a gradual change in attitudes towards brick-and-mortar bookselling, signalling the beginning of a transformation in the field.

Unsurprisingly, booksellers throughout the series are vocal about the effects of Amazon on physical retail. Priyanka Malhotra, the owner of Full Circle, New Delhi, remarks that '[b]ookstores have suffered immensely with online retail giants with deep pockets ... monopolizing the segment'.[128] Ajit Vikram Singh, a former bookseller whose store closed before the pandemic, concurs that readers' clear preference for Amazon's pricing and convenience has led to a 'dark and uncertain' future for the physical bookstore.[129] Multiple booksellers narrate the familiar story of customers photographing books to order online for a lower price.[130] To booksellers, the threat posed by Amazon is clear, and their perspectives are largely a continuation of discussions of 'the death of the bookstore'. More than booksellers' opinions of Amazon, though, the largest impact on brick-and-mortar bookselling arguably comes from the attitudes held by every *other* player in the field; a reduction of Amazon's power would require publishers, distributors, and writers to prioritise the brick-and-mortar bookstore. In this respect, it is worth asking where and how those in the wider publishing field speak about both bookstores and online retail within 'Publishing and the Pandemic'. Once again, going purely by the numbers paints a rosier picture: bookstores were mentioned in 49% of all articles focusing on anglophone trade publishing, and Amazon in only 30%. But

---

[127] Anish Chandy, 'Why the pandemic will lead to a rush of new books on investment, personal finance and start-ups', *Scroll*, 12 November 2020.
[128] Malhotra, 'The pandemic claims an iconic bookshop'.
[129] Ajit Vikram Singh, 'A former bookseller explains why bookshops will find the post-pandemic period especially difficult', *Scroll*, 30 July 2020.
[130] Sheth, 'Mumbai's elegantly curated Wayword & Wise bookshop refuses to go online'.

a mention of brick-and-mortar bookstores does not necessarily reflect an investment in their survival. And, in fact, where individuals in the field apart from booksellers – publishers, distributors and writers, among others – speak of bookstores, this largely consists of an offhand reference to bookstore closures in the pandemic ('online and offline sales have hit rock bottom'[131]). Only 8% of articles by non-booksellers include more than three sentences discussing bookstores; in the overwhelming majority of the dataset, physical bookstores find only a passing mention. In fact, some articles that are framed as surveys of the publishing industry interview, or reference, every agent in the publishing field *except* the bookseller.[132] It would appear that to the industry, bookstores are simultaneously recognised as essential – their closure being worthy of mention by nearly every player in the field – and yet treated as marginal, afforded no extended discussion.

When it comes to Amazon and online retail, on the other hand, publishers, distributors, and authors often have more to say. The owner of a self-publishing platform, for example, asserts that 'more and more authors are realising the benefits of e-commerce over the physical bookstore, and are happy to see their printed books [on] online marketplaces'.[133] In another telling example of Amazon's influence on the wider field, Gaurav Sabharwal, the managing director of Wonder House Books – an imprint set up by Prakash Books, one of India's largest trade distributors – explicitly links his publishing strategy to Amazon:

> There are advantages of having a strong working relationship with [Amazon] – you learn how to make your products

---

[131] Sayantan Ghosh, 'What we talk about when we talk about writing a novel during the pandemic', *Scroll*, 20 June 2020.

[132] See, for instance, Meghna Pant, 'How to get published during the pandemic and afterwards (warning: it will not be easy)', *Scroll*, 2 December 2020. The article discusses authors, literary agents, publishers, self-publishers, and distribution – but not bookselling.

[133] Manish Purohit, 'As publishers face challenges, will self-publishing actually become bigger after the pandemic?', *Scroll*, 10 June 2020.

discoverable on these platforms, you have marketing tools that can influence sales. We rely a lot on data, on what customers are looking for.[134]

In both these cases, Amazon (or online marketplaces more generally) are spoken of in terms of benefits to the publisher, author, and customer; in Sabharwal's framing, Amazon helps publishers better meet readers' demands. Both articles, in fact, speak negatively of the brick-and-mortar bookstore; the interview with Sabharwal links Wonder House's 'success story' to its ability to overcome 'the limitation of bookstores'.[135] Interestingly, Sabharwal refers to Amazon in another article in the series, this time in his capacity as a distributor. Highlighting its detrimental effect on distribution, as Amazon's popularity led to dwindling orders from brick-and-mortar bookstores, Sabharwal nevertheless does not suggest fighting this monopoly; instead, he says, 'as distributors, we can be sellers on Amazon too, if we can figure out how to integrate in the right way'.[136] Rather than challenging the power of Amazon, or supporting brick-and-mortar bookstores, players in the field are willing to invest money in maintaining its status. In another article, the director of the JCB Prize for Literature, one of India's most prestigious literary awards, states matter-of-factly that during the pandemic, when 'the usual elements of real-life promotion in bookshops' were a challenge, the prize simply chose to partner with Amazon.[137] Examples such as these illustrate a field in which Amazon's monopoly is either taken for granted – discussed simply as an immovable feature of the landscape of bookselling – or explicitly supported by members of the industry.

Thus, beyond the direct effects of Amazon's own policies, bookstores are also marginalised as a result of the lack of support within the industry, a theme

---

[134] Selina Sheth, 'How this children's publisher defied the downtrend to boost sales during the pandemic', *Scroll*, 22 August 2021.

[135] Ibid.

[136] Scroll Staff, 'Insider predictions: What does the future of publishing look like after the pandemic?', *Scroll*, 4 January 2021.

[137] Mita Kapur, 'How do you run India's biggest literary prize, the JCB Prize for Literature, in a pandemic year?', *Scroll*, 20 December 2020.

echoed by booksellers across the series. In her account of setting up an independent bookstore in Bengaluru, Radhika Timbadia observes, '[w]hen prestigious literary festivals in India call booksellers from outside India to speak about their experiences, and not anyone within from India ... it makes me wonder whether we can all come together to have a stronger voice and support each other'.[138] The owners of Bahrisons, a set of bookstores in New Delhi, echo these sentiments, stating that a 'bookshop is no singular effort ... It is as much the effort of the bookseller as it is of the author, publisher, salesperson and the reader'.[139] The booksellers at The Book Shop, New Delhi, are much more explicit, declaring that 'the systemic lack of support shown by publishers' is a problem which 'beset[s] the entire bookselling community'.[140] In *Merchants of Culture*, Thompson proposes the idea of the 'polarization of the field', split between a small number of powerful conglomerates and a large number of 'very small publishing operations'.[141] Arguably, a similar kind of 'polarization' manifests in the Indian bookselling field, with a large number of small brick-and-mortar bookstores on the one hand, occupying a relatively marginal place in the overall context of trade publishing and rendered vulnerable by a lack of organisation, visibility, and support; and, on the other hand, a small set of publishers and conglomerates commanding more power.

The idea of a polarised field is further reinforced when considering the one source of consistent support for brick-and-mortar bookstores within this series: independent publishers. The series includes eight articles focusing on independent publishers, all of whom explicitly stress the importance of physical bookstores as 'supportive allies in keeping our work visible and in circulation'.[142] S. Anand, who runs the anti-caste publishing house Navayana, links his titles' visibility in bookstores to his company's higher

[138] Radhika Timbadia, 'Bengaluru's Champaca Bookstore has worked out a model for surviving the pandemic and its aftermath', *Scroll*, 6 August 2020.

[139] Malhotra, 'What led Delhi's Bahrisons to open a new bookshop'.

[140] Chaturvedi and Narain, 'The many ways in which Delhi's The Bookshop reinvented Itself'.

[141] Thompson, *Merchants of Culture*, 146.

[142] Ruby Hembrom, 'Why the pandemic has made little difference to adivaani, Ruby Hembrom's Adivasi publishing house', *Scroll*, 26 May 2020.

'public profile': 'we reach the kind of bookstores that remain out of reach for Dalit publishers'.[143] Yogesh Maitreya, who runs Dalit publishing house Panther's Paw, explains that he has no formal 'distribution mechanism', relying on bookstores for his sales.[144] Frederick Noronha, owner of a niche publishing house in Goa, mentions co-publishing with local bookstores because of the 'reduced risks',[145] and independent publishers Tara Books similarly mitigate risks by operating their own bookstore.[146] While these, too, might be passing mentions, they nevertheless place importance in the varied roles the brick-and-mortar bookstore plays: as an 'ally' for non-mainstream publishing; as a source of visibility and social and symbolic capital; and as an added revenue stream for publishers, through ownership or co-publication. This polarised positioning of the field, and the interdependence between these relatively marginal agents, is an important theme emerging from this series; as will be discussed in the following sections, it is a significant factor which continues to influence the bookselling landscape in 2021 and beyond.

Thus far, these discussions of the brick-and-mortar bookstore might seem somewhat depressing, with threats and vulnerabilities at every turn. But the series also offers a silver lining, documenting evidence of a vital change that takes place over the course of the pandemic, with growing support for the brick-and-mortar bookstore from within the field. In their calls for support, booksellers in the series frequently draw attention to the lack of solidarity within the industry, wondering 'if we can find a way for all of us – authors, publishers, distributors, booksellers and book lovers – to speak to each other, not just as individuals, but as a collective'.[147] One of the

---

[143] S. Anand, 'First person: How Navayana, publisher of anti-caste literature, was born, and where it is going now', *Scroll*, 9 July 2020.

[144] Yogesh Maitreya, 'How Panther's Paw Publications is publishing its Dalit books during, and against, the pandemic', *Scroll*, 4 August 2020.

[145] Frederick Noronha, 'Publishing in the pandemic from a small state: How Goa, 1556 is trying to change the game', *Scroll*, 17 November 2020.

[146] Gita Wolf, 'For Tara Books, maker of handmade books, the road to sustenance in the pandemic has not been easy', *Scroll*, 10 November 2020.

[147] Timbadia, 'Bengaluru's Champaca Bookstore has worked out a model for surviving'.

consequences of the pandemic, in fact, is precisely this; as publisher Priya Kapoor argues, '[a] welcome outcome of the lockdown is that it has sparked more conversations within the publishing industry. In the absence of a robust industry body to bring us together these interactions were infrequent and lacking'.[148] The existence of the series itself exemplifies a long-overdue redressal of some of the gaps in communication and data within the industry, in its efforts to pull together voices from publishing professionals across the country. Within the series, writers frequently reference one another's work, and several of the articles are framed as conversations or roundtables – five months after Radhika Timbadia's plea for people in publishing to 'find a way . . . to speak to each other', she could participate in 'a roundtable with professionals representing every segment of the value chain'.[149] The series also highlights nascent efforts at organisation taking place across the country; Priya Kapoor mentions weekly meetings among publishing professionals, and a group of prominent booksellers advertise their new association for independent bookshops.[150] These emerging displays of organising and solidarity are, in and of themselves, a notable development within the bookselling field.

It is equally important to note that these conversations, in the series and elsewhere, took place at a time in which Amazon's monopoly had been briefly rendered meaningless as a result of restrictions on e-commerce; perhaps for the first time in years, members of the industry were forced to remember the value of the brick-and-mortar bookstore. Bookseller Priyanka Malhotra wryly reflects on this in her account of operating her bookstore in Delhi in 2020:

> During the lockdown, since bookstores were allowed to open before the online retailers . . . we found ourselves being courted by publishers who urged us to open and sell their books . . . some of them were even prepared to offer us

[148] Priya Kapoor, 'For illustrated books, the lockdown makes production difficult. But a digital future brings hope', *Scroll*, 15 May 2020.

[149] Scroll Staff, 'Insider predictions'.

[150] Kapoor, 'For illustrated books'; Gupta, 'Six indie bookstores'.

full marketing and promotional support. ... For a brief period of time, we started feeling as though we were in the pre-online era.[151]

A true restoration of the 'pre-online era' would be impossible; the weakening of Amazon was temporary, and its discounting practices and warehousing infrastructure had already irrevocably altered the field. Still, the publishers' renewed interest in the brick-and-mortar bookstore was a crucial development; and, Malhotra highlights, it extended beyond mere attention and into monetary support. While this moment might not have led to a return to the golden age of physical bookselling, it *did* lead to something new, which would come to define the new logic of the field in 2021 and beyond. The next section explores the ways in which brick-and-mortar bookstores seized this brief advantage by taking a set of actions that would affect their position – in terms of visibility, recognition, and solidarity – and thereby transform the bookselling landscape.

---

[151] Malhotra, 'The pandemic claims an iconic bookshop'.

4 Bookselling in the Pandemic: Independent Bookseller Activism

In parallel to conversations taking place within the industry, as recorded within series such as 'Publishing and the Pandemic', the book trade was taking concrete steps to ensure the survival of their businesses during and beyond the pandemic. For the brick-and-mortar bookstore, this involved finding a way to sell books when physical browsing was difficult or even impossible. What emerged from these efforts was not just a one-off attempt to increase sales, but a long-term campaign aimed at increasing the visibility of the physical bookstore. In *Reluctant Capitalists*, Laura Miller describes the wave of 'independent bookseller activism' in American bookselling in the 1990s, with coordinated movements to protest the monopoly of big-box bookstores, consisting of organising among booksellers; efforts to seek legal protections; and 'educational campaigns' or 'consciousness-raising' activities aimed at gaining public support.[152] This section examines the ways in which bookstores in India began to engage in a form of 'independent bookseller activism' through their use of social media and digital platforms during the pandemic. I argue that this was a key factor in transforming the contemporary bookselling field, by making new forms of online bookselling possible as well as using 'consciousness-raising' tactics to popularise the identity of the independent bookstore, thus allowing for a new culture of solidarity and support for the brick-and-mortar bookstore in India.

This section focuses on two bookstores as primary case studies, both located in metropolitan cities: Bahrisons Booksellers, New Delhi, and Champaca Bookstore, Bengaluru. Champaca, located in south India, was set up in June 2019 as a bookstore, library, and café; the library is restricted to children's books, while the store sells primarily English-language fiction and nonfiction.[153] Bahrisons, in the north, has a much longer history; as its website explains, the bookstore was opened in 1953 'in post-partition India – out of the struggle of one man, who . . . makes new beginnings in a new country by opening his small bookstore in New Delhi's Khan Market'.[154] As of

---

[152] Miller, *Reluctant Capitalists*, 163.

[153] 'About Us', Champaca.

[154] 'About Us', Books at Bahri.

March 2020, Bahrisons had four outlets across Delhi-NCR, including a dedicated children's bookshop; two of the branches had attached cafés.[155] Both bookstores had social media presences before the onset of the pandemic, with accounts on Instagram and Twitter (now X). Bahrisons also had a website, although books had to be ordered via email, and online bookselling was not a primary feature.[156] These bookstores entered the pandemic in very different circumstances: Champaca was barely six months old, whereas Bahrisons had an established position in the field as 'a legendary Delhi landmark'.[157] Nevertheless, both stores turned to social media and digital platforms in similar ways – and with similar effects.

Although I refer to these bookstores' activities as 'independent bookseller activism', it is important to note that the concept of the independent bookstore is itself complex. Miller notes the lack of any 'precise, formal definition' of the independent, but rather a set of themes: small size, 'being locally based and limited in geographic scope'.[158] All of the bookstores discussed so far in this Element fall under this category by definition, but they do not necessarily self-identify or advertise themselves as independent bookstores. Bahrisons, for example, continues to describe themselves as a 'family-run bookshop' on their official Instagram and website.[159] Similarly, Champaca announced its opening on Instagram with hashtags such as '#newbookstore' and '#bookcafe', rather than alluding to 'independence'.[160] Miller argues that the 'identity of independence, with its corresponding sense of solidarity' only emerged in the United States in response to the rise of chain bookstores.[161] I suggest that a similar emergence and communication of a collective identity is a key

---

[155] Bahrisons Booksellers (Bahrisons_booksellers), 'It's getting very warm in Delhi', Instagram, 25 May 2020.

[156] See 'Home', Books at Bahri, archived on 8 October 2019.

[157] Mayank Austen Soofi, 'Delhiwale: The Khan Market matriarch', *Hindustan Times*, 15 July, 2019.

[158] Miller, *Reluctant Capitalists*, 165.

[159] Bahrisons Booksellers (@bahrisons_booksellers), Instagram; 'About Us', Books at Bahri.

[160] Champaca Books (champacabooks), 'The bookshelves have appeared on the book wall!', Instagram, 6 May, 2019.

[161] Miller, *Reluctant Capitalists*, 165.

feature of bookstores' activity over the course of the pandemic. In exploring these case studies, I also draw upon other examples of bookstores in the country who used social media in similar ways, acknowledging both the networked and interactive nature of what Kenna MacTavish calls the 'post-digital book world'[162] as well as the coordinated efforts across the country that were necessary in building and sustaining this activism.

4.1 Beyond Brick-and-Mortar: Bookselling Online

In 'Crisis Book Browsing: Restructuring the Retail Shelf Life of Books', Kenna MacTavish explores the ways that independent bookstores in Australia responded to the pandemic as they shifted from being sites of browsing to 'solely fulfilment warehouses', arguing that social media became a 'lifeline for independent bookstores'.[163] In India, too, bookstores used the initial months of the pandemic to harness social media and digital platforms in new ways. As of March 2020, online bookselling was not a primary feature of many brick-and-mortar bookstores, especially stand-alones; nor did India have initiatives such as Bookshop.org.[164] Bookstores therefore faced the task of expanding their sales capacities to an entirely new sphere, innovating new practices, as well as educating customers on how to order books online.

Both Bahrisons and Champaca used Instagram as a primary platform to communicate these developments. Bahrisons chose to advertise through a series of detailed, text-based posts. On 2 May 2020, they announced that they would be opening to deliveries; over the next two days, two more posts on their feed explained the new ordering process. Customers had to place their orders by telephone; orders would then be delivered by the store, or

---

[162] MacTavish, 'Crisis book browsing', 53. I follow MacTavish's use of the term 'post-digital book world', which she sees as emphasising the 'material interplay' between social media and physical bookselling practices in contrast to the 'born-digital' environments suggested by terms such as the digital literary sphere (53).

[163] Ibid.

[164] Bookshop.org was launched in January 2020 as 'an alternative to Amazon for socially-conscious online shoppers', working as a storefront for independent bookstores in the United States and later the UK and Spain; see 'About Us', Bookshop.org.

customers could arrange for pick-up via a third-party delivery service.[165] While orders were initially restricted to a limited number of neighbourhoods, a few days later, on 11 May, Bahrisons posted that they were open to deliveries throughout Delhi.[166] A few weeks later, on 1 June, a new post announced: 'The news you have been waiting for – we are now able to send books all over the country.'[167] This time, the order instructions included an email address and a list of required details for the order; the caption also instructed customers, 'Don't DM [direct message] on Instagram!'[168] These frequent, text-heavy posts are an awkward addition to a primarily visually appealing Instagram feed, suggesting a degree of unfamiliarity on the part of both bookseller and consumer; they reflect in real time the bookstore's own processes of streamlining online sales systems as well as the need to educate customers on specific steps of coordinating order, payment, and delivery. For its part, Champaca avoided some of these challenges by making a more drastic decision: they used the period of total lockdown to create an online store, which was launched on 4 May 2020. The store was announced on Instagram in a post captioned inviting readers to '[b]uy a book from our specially-curated online store'.[169] For the first two weeks, Champaca only delivered within the city; two weeks later, on May 26, a post on their Instagram feed announced: 'Delivering across India', with a long caption explaining their vision for the webstore:

> Our little team has been hard at work this past month to
> bring the unique book-buying experience of Champaca

---

[165] Bahrisons Booksellers (Bahrisons_booksellers), 'Missing your favourite bookstore?'. Instagram, 3 May, 2020; Bahrisons Booksellers (Bahrisons_booksellers), 'More good news for book lovers!', Instagram, 4 May 2020.

[166] Bahrisons Booksellers (Bahrisons_booksellers), 'Good news Delhi readers', Instagram, 11 May 2020.

[167] Bahrisons Booksellers (Bahrisons_booksellers), 'The news you have been waiting for', Instagram, 1 June 2020.

[168] Ibid.

[169] Champaca Books (champacabooks), 'Champaca is open for pick-up', Instagram, 4 May 2020.

> online. ... It may be on the web instead of our verdant space, but our focus on bringing you specially curated collections, and books from a range of independent Indian publishers remains unchanged.[170]

While Bahrisons encouraged readers to place orders via email or phone, Champaca's new website offered a browse-and-buy experience that might appear more recognisable and seamless to consumers used to platforms like Amazon. In both cases, though, the bookstores continued to use social media to advertise their online offerings, as well as to communicate changes in delivery capacities as lockdown restrictions continued to fluctuate. Both stores also reminded customers of the newness of these structures: 'we hope you will be patient ... while we iron out all the small glitches', read the caption to Champaca's post launching deliveries across India;[171] and Bahrisons similarly asked their Instagram followers to understand that 'at times we may get a little delayed ... but will definately [*sic*] get back to you'.[172] These reminders of the human effort behind bookstores' new online processes exemplifies what MacTavish calls 'a post-digital book world rationale',[173] combining the familiar aspects of online sales with the equally familiar idiosyncrasies of brick-and-mortar browsing and buying experiences.

The brick-and-mortar experience is, of course, a key feature differentiating the bookstore from an e-retailer; and, as bookstores made the shift to online bookselling, they were also striving to transfer the experience of the physical bookstore to the online sphere. MacTavish introduces the term 'crisis book browsing' to describe 'the rapid shift in book browsing practices as a result of ongoing global crises', looking at Australian bookstores' use of social media to recreate specific experiences of their physical stores.[174] In India, too, these shifts had begun to appear. On 20 May 2020, Bahrisons

---

[170] Champaca Books (champacabooks), 'Champaca is now delivering across India', Instagram, 26 May 2020.

[171] Ibid.

[172] Bahrisons Booksellers (Bahrisons_booksellers), 'Hello readers', Instagram, 26 July 2020.

[173] MacTavish, 'Crisis book browsing', 54. [174] Ibid., 51.

announced a new initiative on Instagram, 'An afternoon with Bahrisons', offering customers appointment-only video calls in which 'a dedicated staff member' would provide 'uninterrupted browsing' of the store's extensive design and cooking sections.[175] Champaca, in turn, emphasised their in-store curation, which they aimed to make available online. Their website was organised to reflect this; as of 2020, for example, customers could browse through selections such as 'Bangalore Authors', 'Caste', 'Zines', and 'Books About Books', as well as collections spotlighting local independent presses such as Seagull, Zubaan, and Navayana.[176] In June 2020, Champaca extended its curation to a new format, announcing the Champaca Book Subscription, a themed monthly subscription box accompanied by an online book club.[177] In addition, throughout 2020, the store hosted a range of online events directly on the Instagram platform, as well as on Zoom, which retained elements of the in-store experience; the offerings in June, for example, included a cooking session with the chef from their instore café and an online version of their customary literary quiz.[178] In a variety of ways, then, both bookstores were working to extend facets of their brick-and-mortar experience to their online platforms.

The previous examples of bookstores' use of social media and digital bookselling centre two primary experiences: allowing customers to virtually access the physical spaces of the bookstore, and transferring the selection and display practices of the physical store into its online proxy in a post-digital book world. This emphasis on curation, Ann Steiner argues, is one of the vital functions of the bookshop; as she observes, 'the experience and sensation' of a bookstore is as much a product as the books on sale.[179] Nor

---

[175] Bahrisons Booksellers (Bahrisons_booksellers), 'An afternoon at Bahrisons', Instagram, 20 May 2020.

[176] 'Collections', Champaca, archived on 22 July 2020.

[177] Champaca Books (champacabooks), 'We're terribly excited to announce our latest adventure', Instagram, 7 June 2020.

[178] Champaca Books (champacabooks), 'We hope to see you for our online events in June', Instagram, 3 June 2020.

[179] Ann Steiner, 'Select, display, and sell: Curation practices in the bookshop', *Logos* 28, no. 4 (March 2017): 18.

were Bahrisons and Champaca alone in this effort; bookstores across the country were focused on transferring the unique 'experience and sensation' of their brick-and-mortar environments to the online sphere, in varying ways. The Book Shop, Jor Bagh in New Delhi encouraged readers to order via Instagram, which they had long used as a platform to interact with customers, rather than setting up a website for sales.[180] At the other end of the spectrum, Atta Galatta – a bookstore in Bengaluru specialising in Indian anglophone titles – chose *not* to sell online, in the belief that that 'the core of our bookstore would [be] squelched by the unfeeling, all-seeing Internet'.[181] Instead, they used social media solely for book-related conversations, offering recommendations and featuring interviews with authors and readers.[182] For the most part, though, bookstores responded to the pandemic by quickly transitioning to online bookselling, whether via Instagram, WhatsApp, or website – resulting in a bookselling field where, for the first time, readers who wanted to order a book from the comfort of their homes were presented with far more options than just Amazon or Flipkart.[183] At the same time, in emphasising the unique experiences of their individual stores, these booksellers were effecting a second, even more paradigm-shifting transformation of the field.

4.2 'Thank You for Supporting Independent Bookstores!': Activism and Identity

Even as bookstores made online bookselling possible, sales were not guaranteed. As MacTavish notes, bookstores using social media suffer an

---

[180] Chaturvedi and Narain, 'The many ways in which Delhi's The Bookshop reinvented itself'.

[181] Sankar, 'What the pandemic means for this independent bookstore'.

[182] See Atta Galatta – The Bookstore (attagalatta), Instagram. The bookstore did, however, allow customers within the city to order via phone and organise delivery via a third-party app.

[183] Significantly, the articles within 'Publishing and the Pandemic' also illustrate that this transition was not restricted to metropolitan cities, but extended across the country, including non-anglophone bookstores and those in smaller cities and regions, which began to offer sales via WhatsApp or other online platforms.

algorithmic disadvantage, with little control over visibility on third-party platforms; they must rely on community engagement (or paid promotions, which are likely unaffordable).[184] For this reason, bookstores' use of social media for 'consciousness-raising' is particularly important, as a means to build not just visibility, but a sense of community and a culture of support. In India, this consciousness-raising took the form of creating and communicating the identity of the independent bookstore.

Looking at both case studies, the 'independent' identity is notably quick to emerge in the early months of the pandemic. This is perhaps most interesting in the case of Bahrisons; despite its nearly seventy-year history, the bookstore rarely branded itself as an independent bookstore before 2020, and did not use the phrase in a single Instagram post throughout 2019.[185] Almost immediately after the lockdowns began, though, the term began to appear: on 5 May, a post thanked customers for their 'continued trust, support and loyalty to independent bookstores like us'.[186] Two days later, an even more succinct image on their feed simply read: 'Thank you for supporting independent bookstores!'[187] Bahrisons' choice to explicitly, and repeatedly, brand themselves as an independent bookstore for the first time amidst this fresh wave of online activity suggests that there was new value in embracing this identity. One reason might be the boost in the visibility of the term, thanks to bookstores across the country participating in this new consciousness-raising. Nearly every post on Champaca's Instagram feed across 2020 used the term 'independent bookstore' in either the image, caption or both; they also went a step further, explaining to readers the necessity and value of supporting independent bookstores. This messaging began very early on; on 19 March 2020, before formal lockdowns had even begun, Champaca posted a photo of their bookselling team on

---

[184] MacTavish, 'Crisis book browsing', 52–53.

[185] Bahrisons Booksellers (Bahrisons_booksellers), Instagram. The phrase 'independent bookstore' does appear three times in 2019, but only in reposts of other users' photos.

[186] Bahrisons Booksellers (Bahrisons_booksellers), 'What are you reading-have you placed your order yet?', Instagram, 5 May 2020.

[187] Bahrisons Booksellers (Bahrisons_booksellers), 'Thank you to all our customers and readers for all the love and support', Instagram, 7 May 2020.

Instagram, announcing that they would be temporarily closing the store out of a concern for health and safety. The caption read, 'we're a newly opened independent bookstore, and closing our doors makes it difficult for us … to cover costs, rents, salaries', asking customers to buy a gift voucher to support them during this time.[188] On 14 April 2020, they reiterated: 'By buying gift vouchers and spreading the word … you have strengthened our belief that books and independent bookstores are essential to the fabric of our lives.'[189] Throughout the periods of lockdown across 2020 and 2021, posts on their Instagram asked readers to 'Order online from your favourite independent bookstore' and 'Support your favourite independent bookstore', frequently in combination with photographs of the team, reminding followers of the people behind the physical and virtual storefronts: as one caption read, 'Champaca is what it is because of the hard work and unflagging enthusiasm that [our team] bring to the space, whether online or offline.'[190] More explicitly than Bahrisons, Champaca also spoke of the independent bookstore as a collective identity defined in opposition to e-commerce sites: '[b]uying books from an independent bookstore, instead of Amazon, can make a world of difference for your local booksellers'.[191] In this manifestation of social media usage, brick-and-mortar bookstores can be seen to adopt a range of strategies. On the one hand, the melding of online and offline elements extends the 'post-digital book world rationale'.[192] At the same time, it also reflects a sustained and careful rhetorical positioning – after all, none of these social media posts acknowledge the fact that e-commerce giants like Amazon, too, were staffed by human beings whose

[188] Champaca Books (champacabooks), 'We've closed Champaca for a week till March 23rd', Instagram, 19 March 2020.

[189] Champaca Books (champacabooks), 'We want to say a big and heartfelt thank you to everyone who has supported us through this lockdown!', Instagram, 14 April 2020.

[190] Champaca Books (champacabooks), 'You can order books online from Champaca, your favourite independent bookstore', Instagram, 21 February 2021; Champaca Books (champacabooks), 'As the public health crisis worsens …', Instagram, 24 April 2021; Champaca Books (champacabooks), 'This Diwali, meet the Champaca team', Instagram, 14 November 2020.

[191] Champaca Books (Champacabooks), 'As the public health crisis worsens …'.

[192] MacTavish, 'Crisis Book Browsing', 54.

livelihoods were affected by the pandemic. Instead, in aligning independent bookstores *with* local communities, and *against* a faceless, capitalist e-commerce site, these bookstores were actively constructing a powerful narrative of a collective identity.

This identity-building, particularly the explicit articulation of an opposition to Amazon, is a form of independent bookseller activism that most vividly echoes across brick-and-mortar bookstores' online presences in 2020 and 2021. In August 2021, for example, Storyteller Bookstore, Kolkata, posted a thread on X explaining the challenges long faced by independent bookstores, such as authors' and publishers' tendency to publicise Amazon links for their new releases.[193] The post was reposted by Bookworm Bookstore, Bengaluru, who added: 'Support independent bookstores ... We are all part of the community, your community', and went on to name specific bookstores, including Champaca.[194] In a separate thread, Bookworm listed the advantages that independent bookstores offered, observing that their role was to 'be of service to the readers & authors as part of the community'.[195] In this way, brick-and-mortar bookstores were creating, and sustaining, a conversation about their own identity. By amplifying one another's voices, they were exhibiting a visible solidarity and sense of community, forging ties across a scattered, disconnected brick-and-mortar landscape – and the effects of this activism were almost immediately visible, in the form of more sustained support for the brick-and-mortar bookstore from others within the field.

4.3 'At a Bookstore Near You': Support and Solidarity

As bookstores' independent bookseller activism grew more visible and coordinated, publishers began to join the conversation, using their own

---

[193] Storyteller Bookstore (Storytellerkol), 'As independent bookshops, one has no leverage and has to always be at the mercy of book suppliers', X, 15 August 2021.

[194] Bookworm Bookstore, Blr (bookworm_Kris), 'Support independent bookstores', X, 16 August 2021.

[195] Bookworm Bookstore, Blr (bookworm_Kris), 'All independent bookstores like us get such questions', X, 8 February 2022.

digital platforms to express support. Naturally, this began in the period in which e-commerce sites could not sell books. As early as April 2020, HarperCollins India posed a thread on X, listing bookstores that were open for delivery.[196] Penguin India posted a similar thread in May 2020, although this list was restricted to bookstores in Delhi-NCR.[197] These instances are more utilitarian, as publishers were forced to rely on bookstores as their only platform for sales. However, other efforts by publishers were more long-lasting. For example, from May 2020 onwards, HarperCollins India began to advertise its new releases on X with the phrase 'available online or at a bookstore near you'; while this is standard practice in other markets, prior to 2020, announcements were only accompanied by an e-commerce link, with no mention of a physical bookstore.[198] This is, admittedly, still a fairly cosmetic change – the clickable link on each post still leads to Amazon – but indicates a rhetorical reprioritisation on the part of publishers. As well, these publishers' accounts had far more followers and greater visibility than those of independent bookstores; their mentions of the brick-and-mortar bookstores, however minor, were essential in communicating their existence and importance to a wider audience.

Beyond support for physical bookstores in general, publishers also began to engage more prominently with the 'independent' identity. In late April 2020, HarperCollins India launched a video series on YouTube, 'ShopTalk', a 'series with indie bookstores'.[199] The first episode, featuring Bahrisons, is titled 'Shop Around the Corner' – a reference that recalls the independent bookstore in the 1998 film *You've Got Mail*, perhaps the most well-known depiction of the indie-versus-chain conflict in popular culture. The reference might have been unintentional, but it is fitting, as Bahrisons and other brick-and-mortar bookstores used the months following the

---

[196] HarperCollins (HarperCollinsIN), 'We're so delighted that indie bookstores are opening slowly but surely', X, 29 April 2020.

[197] Penguin India (PenguinIndia), 'Good news for those of you who need to breathe in the new-book smell of paper and ink!', X, 2 May 2020.

[198] See HarperCollins (HarperCollinsIN), X.

[199] Harper Broadcast (HarperBroadcast), *#ShopTalk | Episode 1 | Shop around the Corner, Bahrisons Booksellers*, YouTube, 24 April, 2020.

pandemic to engage in their own form of independent bookseller activism. And although the results were not immediate, by the time the pandemic restrictions had eased, the bookselling field had dramatically transformed – with the brick-and-mortar bookstore experiencing, not a death, but a long-awaited renaissance.

5 New Field, New Logics: The Brick-and-Mortar Bookstore in Post-Pandemic India

As I have attempted to illustrate across my analysis, the brick-and-mortar bookstore occupied a relatively marginal position in the field at the start of the pandemic, but a growing movement of independent bookseller activism online, combined with more recognition from the industry, helped to strengthen their visibility and build networks of support. Although this activism was undoubtedly effective in bringing attention to the brick-and-mortar bookstore in 2020 and 2021, the question remained: as pandemic restrictions eased, and Amazon returned to regular operations, would the 'death of the bookstore' simply pick up where it left off? On the contrary, an examination of the bookselling landscape from 2021 to the time of this writing, in August 2024, reveals that the brick-and-mortar bookstore has not only weathered the pandemic, but is thriving; and, for the first time since the introduction of Amazon, the bookselling field seems to have been fundamentally altered. This section explores some of the new logics of this revitalised field of contemporary bookselling: an expanded network of brick-and-mortar and independent bookstores; the implications of this new landscape for bibliodiversity in Indian publishing; and the changing corporate and conglomerate priorities which help to promote the revival of physical bookstores.

5.1 The Post-Pandemic Bookselling Landscape

As pandemic restrictions eased and the world entered its 'new normal', the bookselling landscape of 2021 looked very different than it had even two years ago. The conversations built around supporting independent bookstores could not mitigate all the challenges bookstores faced, and closures were inevitable, including for several of the bookshops featured in 'Publishing and the Pandemic'. In Hyderabad, Walden – once a thriving chain in the city, which in its heyday had boasted popcorn machines and make-your-own-T-shirt counters – closed their last remaining outlet in October 2020; Mohan's Bookshop in Kolkata shut in May 2021.[200] Beyond this, of course, are the

---

[200] Sheth, 'Walden, Hyderabad (1990–2020)'; Datta, 'How Kolkata's famous Mohan's Bookshop lost its battle'.

bookstores whose existence was not recorded in this series or elsewhere. Nevertheless, even as lockdowns and social distancing continued through to early 2022, it seemed that more bookstores were opening doors, rather than closing them. Both bookstores focused on in my case studies opened new outlets: Bahrisons launched a new store in New Delhi in October 2020, while lockdowns were still in place, and in the next two years they expanded beyond Delhi-NCR for the first time, with a store in Chandigarh in April 2022, followed by one in Kolkata in 2023.[201] Champaca, too, opened a new branch in Goa in October 2022.[202] For both bookstores, this was a notable development: the former an established, nearly seventy-year-old institution, expanding to other states for the first time; and the latter a brand-new store, capable of growth within three years of operation. Elsewhere, too, new beginnings abounded: Full Circle addressed the challenge of higher rent by moving to a new location in 2020; Pagdandi Bookstore Café in Pune opened a new branch in 2022; and Walking Bookfairs opened doors in Cuttack in 2023.[203] Other stores saw a more literal rebirth: The Book Shop, an iconic Delhi bookstore, announced its closure in October 2023, but swiftly rebranded as The Bookshop Inc., with 'a new partnership, a new location, a new adventure'.[204] Stand-alone stores were not the only ones expanding; in August 2023, STORY, a Kolkata chain, relocated to 'a sprawling 4,000 sq feet bookstore', and opened a second outlet the following month.[205] And Crossword, India's largest chain, opened its

---

[201] Malhotra, 'What led Delhi's Bahrisons to open a new bookshop'; 'New In the City: Get booked', *Indian Express*, 10 April 2022; Bahrisons Bookseller (Bahrisons_books), 'Kolkata-We are in your town now!', X, 18 January 2023.

[202] Champaca Books (champacabooks), 'We're branching out of our leafy home in Bangalore – and opening a bookstore in a new state!', Instagram, 25 October 2022.

[203] Malhotra, 'The pandemic claims an iconic bookshop'; Dipanita Nath, 'Pune Inc: How a bookstore is taking on e-commerce giants by focussing on old-fashioned reading habits', *Indian Express*, 8 November 2022; Walking Bookfairs (walkingbookfairs), 'We made a beautiful new bookstore for you', Instagram, October 2 2023.

[204] Priyanjali Malik, 'Farewell to the Bookshop', *The Wire*, 31 October, 2023.

[205] Vedant Karia, 'STORY bookstore returns with a grand palatial look in Salt Lake', *Telegraph*, 11 August 2023; Vedant Karia, 'STORY opens doors in New Town', *Telegraph*, 23 September 2023.

one hundredth branch in the country in 2023.[206] For the brick-and-mortar bookstore, whether independents or chains, it seemed that the post-pandemic environment offered new possibilities for expansion and growth.

The visibility of these bookstores in online spaces might have helped them survive and expand their reach. Even more interesting, though, is the emergence of brand-new bookstores across the country, which were able to benefit from this wave of independent bookseller activism. In Kohima in northeast India, an independent bookstore and café called The Common Room opened in late 2020.[207] Hyderabad lost an iconic bookstore in 2020, but in 2022 Luna, a 'cosy and serene independent bookstore', opened its doors.[208] The same year, The White Owl Book Lounge opened in Nagaland in northeast India, promising to 'transcend the conventional boundaries of a mere bookshop', with a 'carefully curated selection' for every reader.[209] As recently as January 2023, a 'bistro and bookstore', Casa Kundera, was set up in Dehradun in north India.[210] Amidst this flurry of growth, existing businesses were even choosing to pivot to bookselling. Kunzum Travel Café, a well-known café in Delhi, announced an ambitious rebrand on its website in early 2022:

> The popular Kunzum Travel Cafe will now be a place to buy books. . . . But the collections will be carefully curated – even as we retain the coffee, the events and the sense of community.[211]

A set of infographics explains the new concept: 'It's a chain of bookshops! It's a café! It's a community', describing their reimagined space as a '(bricks &

---

[206] Crossword Bookstores (crossword_book), '100 stores, countless happy book-lovers!', X, 8 September 2023.

[207] Vishü Rita Krocha, 'The Common Room, turning a new page amid the pandemic', *Morung Express*, 14 September 2020.

[208] Sruthi Kuruganti, 'Here's a new place for bibliophiles in Hyderabad to explore', *Telangana Today*, 27 October 2022.

[209] 'Who we are', The White Owl.   [210] See Casa Kundera (casakundera), X.

[211] 'About', Kunzum.

mortar) place where authors, readers, editors, designers, publishers ... come together'.[212] Kunzum debuted its new identity by opening five stores across the city over two months – including one outlet, called Penguin@Kunzum, described as 'the world's only exclusive store showcasing the best of the world's biggest publisher!'[213] Kunzum's reinvention perhaps best illustrates the transformation that has taken place in the field: with an established business choosing to pivot to bookselling on such a large scale; the 'independent' rhetoric of curation, community, and physical space running throughout its mission statement; and the clear industry support evidenced by the involvement of a 'big five' publisher, Penguin Random House India.

This spate of new openings and expansion – a phenomenon which had not been seen in India since the 'golden age' of the chain nearly two decades ago – does have its parallels in other post-pandemic book markets. In the United States, 300 new independent bookstores opened between 2020 and 2022, 'in a surprising and welcome revival'.[214] The American chain, too, seems to be thriving, with Barnes & Noble poised to open fifty new outlets in 2024.[215] The UK also saw expansion in brick-and-mortar bookstores in 2023, although this was accompanied by more closures of independent bookstores.[216] As well, outside of the major anglophone markets, different book markets saw varying, often surprising changes in the wake of the pandemic. In Argentina, Buenos Aires, known for its rich bookselling landscape, saw bookstores 'multiplying and thriving' through the pandemic, despite economic instability – to the point that booksellers have begun to worry about an 'oversaturation' of the market.[217] At the other end of the

---

[212] 'Bookshops', Kunzum.

[213] 'About', Kunzum.

[214] Alexandra Alter and Elizabeth A. Harris, 'Some surprising good news: Bookstores are booming and becoming more diverse', *The New York Times*, 10 July 2022.

[215] Jim Milliot, 'Following a successful 2023, B&N aims to open 50 stores in 2024', *Publishers Weekly*, 10 January 2024.

[216] Heloise Wood, 'BA describes "volatile year" for bookshop openings and closures', *The Bookseller*, 5 January 2024.

[217] Daniel Politi, 'Through a recession and a pandemic, the book business is thriving in Buenos Aires', *The New York Times*, 26 May 2022.

spectrum, both Brazil – where leading bookstore chains had already suffered before 2020 – and South Africa saw the pandemic push more readers away from bookstores, towards digital reading and e-commerce sites such as Amazon.[218] And in the Philippines, the expansion of online sales took a slightly different route, as publishers began to bypass bookstores entirely, and deal directly with customers.[219] These different developments are testament to the unique infrastructural, economic, and cultural contexts of each book market; while some of the factors prompting growth in countries such as the United States and the UK doubtless apply in the Indian context – such as falling rents in the wake of the pandemic – others, most notably governmental support for physical bookstores, did not occur in the Indian context.[220] India has seen the beginning of some forms of organisation, such as the Independent Bookshops Association of India (IBAI), although this is still in early stages, and as of August 2024 only involves sixteen bookstores as members.[221] Nevertheless, it seems clear that, as a collective, the brick-and-mortar bookstore no longer faces the same degree of marginalisation and vulnerability that were so evident over the last decade. As a more visible, robust network, this also means that brick-and-mortar bookstores can exert more influence on the wider context of trade publishing.

5.2 Bibliodiversity and the Bookstore

In 2015, feminist publisher Urvashi Butalia remarked upon one of the consequences of the 'death of the bookstore', worrying that '[b]ibliodiversity is in

---

[218] Trini Vergara, Frankfurt Book Fair 2023: Brazil's Skeelo looks to go global', *Publishers Weekly*, 20 October 2023; Elizabeth le Roux, Savannah Harvett, and Lezli Edgar, *South African Book Publishing Industry Survey 2022–23* (Cape Town: Publishers' Association of South Africa, 2024).

[219] Beatriz Marie D. Cruz, 'Publishers, bookshops ride the digital wave spurred by pandemic', *Business World*, 20 December 2023.

[220] Alter and Harris, 'Some surprising good news'.

[221] See 'Become a member', Independent Bookshops Association of India. It should be noted that their membership criteria – which specify that stores 'should earn not less than 60% of ... revenue from the sale of general trade books if other items such as stationery [are sold] or if a cafe is operated' – might exclude many of the bookstore-cafés which have opened in recent months.

danger'.[222] 'Bibliodiversity' – a term created by Chilean independent publishers, and popularised by Susan Hawthorne – emphasises the role of independent publishers in 'contribut[ing] to a thriving life of culture'.[223] Butalia used the word more generally, speaking of the effect of Amazon's power in boosting sales of bestsellers, to the detriment of midlist or unknown titles – another kind of flattening of the range of voices that are given space and publicity.[224] In both senses, however, the revival of the bookstore, and specifically of the independent bookstore, is a positive sign for bibliodiversity in contemporary Indian publishing.

As discussed earlier, independent presses in the country have long been reliant on bookstores, rather than online platforms, for their survival. A more diverse landscape of independent bookstores, therefore, has only increased the possibility for visibility and promotion of a wider range of titles. Part of this is simply due to the fact that, in a newly populated landscape, and amidst the wave of independent bookseller activism, brick-and-mortar bookstores must increasingly stress the curatorial value of their individual selections in order to stand out in the crowd. Champaca's website, for example, allows customers to browse individual independent publishers, including a range of Indian presses such as Kokaachi, Reliable Copy, and Adivaani.[225] Luna Books in Hyderabad does not offer a webstore, but states on its website that their team is 'mindful of ensuring diversity – in vintage, genre ... and authorship' in its selection of books.[226] As well, recent years have seen bookstores leverage their new visibility by supporting independent publishers and local writers in other ways; in 2021, for example, *Scroll* reported that Pagdandi, Pune, was 'in preliminary talks with a few indie publishers to increase the print runs of certain books based on orders'.[227] Other efforts are

---

[222] Chandrasekaran, 'The death of the bookstore'.
[223] Susan Hawthorne, 'Bibliodiversity: Creating content or invigorating culture?', *Logos* 27, no. 1 (June 2016): 63. Interestingly, Hawthorne also cites Butalia's early 'iteration' of the idea of bibliodiversity (65).
[224] Chandrasekaran, 'The death of the bookstore'.
[225] 'Collections', Champaca.
[226] 'Luna: the neighbourhood bookstore', Luna Books.
[227] Arunima Mazumdar, 'Why Pagdandi of Pune transformed its library-cum-cafe into a bookstore during the pandemic', *Scroll*, 1 August 2021.

on an even larger scale, involving multiple stakeholders: in Nagaland, the White Owl bookstore launched The White Owl Literature Festival and Book Fair in February 2024 in collaboration with Penguin Random House and Cambridge University Press, aiming to celebrate 'the Northeast's history, culture and geography'.[228] In their curation and championing of local voices and independent presses, bookstores can promote bibliodiversity in a variety of ways.

A diversity of titles is important, but in a country with such a historically fragmented, uneven bookselling landscape, it is perhaps equally important to cultivate a readership; central to the idea of bibliodiversity is the idea of a culture or ecosystem that is as dependent on consumers as it is on producers. As accounts across 'Publishes and the Pandemic' highlighted, in several parts of the country, visiting a physical bookstore was a rarity even as recently as 2020; and it is important to acknowledge the ways in which the brick-and-mortar bookstore, and particularly the independent bookstore, can appear to be an intimidating, elitist, or exclusive space – or at the very least an unfamiliar one. I suggest that another way in which the revival of brick-and-mortar bookselling can contributed to greater bibliodiversity is through encouraging reading and book-buying cultures. In recent years, brick-and-mortar bookstores have taken steps to make themselves more accessible to a wider readership by reimagining the space and function of the bookstore. Between late 2023 and early 2024, for example, multiple bookstores, including Dogears, Goa; Pagdandi, Pune; and Kunzum, Delhi, set up book clubs, with readers free to bring their own books rather than making purchases.[229] Several bookstores, such as Champaca, Kunzum, The White Owl, and The Common Room also double as lending libraries, thus making at least part of their collections

---

[228] 'The White Owl Literature Festival & Book Fair: A literary extravaganza in the heart of Nagaland', The White Owl.

[229] See, for example, Pagdandi bookstore café (pagdandi), 'The reading circle is back at Pagdandi!', Instagram, 13 September 2023; The Dogears Bookshop (the_dogears_bookshop), 'Putting this out here', Instagram, 22 January 2024; 'Kunzum book clubs', Kunzum.

available to a wider readership who might not be able to afford new books at full price.[230]

At the same time, as a result of the independent bookseller activism across the pandemic, these efforts have been matched by a greater awareness among consumers, which also serves to diversify readership and reading cultures. Laura Miller suggests that conscious consumerism is a key factor in supporting independent bookstores, 'provid[ing] a means to exercise influence in economic processes that generally appear beyond the control of ordinary people'.[231] The extreme price-sensitivity of the Indian market makes conscious consumer choices a complex subject; nevertheless, the rhetoric of ethical consumption and supporting local bookstores has noticeably increased since 2020, perhaps supported by the rising education levels and digital access of India's growing young population.[232] The Reddit community 'Indianbooks', for example, has seen multiple discussions between 2020 and 2022 asking for recommendations of 'ethical' places to buy books in India.[233] And, in the absence of a database of bookstores in the country, readers have stepped in to fill in these gaps: in June 2022, blogger Peter Griffin posted a crowd-sourced map, 'Indie bookshops in India', inspired by a conversation with bookseller (and IBAI founder) Leonard Fernandes.[234] Users were asked to contribute by adding trade bookstores to the map; as of August 2024, the map includes 132 bookstores.[235] And, while gauging the actual impact of these shifts in

---

[230] 'The Champaca Children's Library', Champaca; 'How it works', Kunzum; 'Who we are', The White Owl; The Common Room (__thecommonroom__), Instagram.

[231] Miller, *Reluctant Capitalists*, 229. [232] Mathur, 'Frankfurt Book Fair 2022'.

[233] See, for example, 'I am trying to move away from Amazon and Audible for books since I find Amazon's work ethics questionable', r/indianbooks, Reddit, 2020; 'Is there an ethical place to buy books from?', r/indianbooks, Reddit, 2022; 'Support independent bookshops', r/indianbooks, Reddit, 2022.

[234] Peter Griffin, 'Indie bookshops in India', zigzackly's omnium-gatherum, 7 June, 2022.

[235] Users are encouraged to add bookstores which stock books in English or regional languages; however, these must fulfil the IBAI's definition of 'independent bookstore', which excludes stores with attached cafés.

consumer behaviour is notoriously difficult, sales data has been promising. In 2023, Nielsen's mid-year update on international markets reported growth in India, citing 'consumers ... embracing a return to bricks-and-mortar stores'.[236] This growth has continued through 2024, with India displaying the highest growth amongst sixteen markets surveyed.[237]

In this way, the post-pandemic bookselling landscape is bibliodiverse in the most multifaceted sense of the word, with brick-and-mortar bookstores forming a vital part of an ecosystem, providing a set of new, varied spaces in which readers can access a range of books by local and independent authors, interact, and form community. In turn, this might suggest the possibility of a change in the polarisation of the field, with growing recognition for both the brick-and-mortar bookstore and the independent press, which were previously marginalised and relatively powerless. However, while the bookstore (and independent presses) might be flourishing in the contemporary field, their revival remains inextricably linked to the priorities and decisions of other bigger, and more influential, players in the field.

5.3 Conglomerate and Corporate Priorities: The End of the Age of Amazon?

As the brick-and-mortar bookstore transformed from a marginal, vulnerable entity to a growing, thriving space, it did not do so in a vacuum; the positions and priorities of other individuals and organisations in the field were also affected by the pandemic in important ways, impacting the wider industry. In this case, a key element of the new logic of the field comes from exploring the changing priorities of conglomerate publishers, and their relationship to another corporate giant: Amazon. Alongside their own activism, the revival of the brick-and-mortar bookstore is equally afforded by conglomerate

---

[236] Hazel Kenyon, 'Frankfurt Book Fair 2023: Tracking trends in international book sales', *Publishers Weekly*, 19 October 2023.

[237] 'Global Book Market 2024 shaped by strong fiction, declining non-fiction and slower price increases', *Nielsen*, 15 October 2024. It should be noted that this press release does not provide any data on the proportion of physical retail to online sales.

publishers' decision to reinvest value in bookstores – which, in turn, might be a consequence of their own changing relationship with Amazon.

To begin with, it is worth briefly outlining how conglomerate publishing functions in the Indian context. While the anglophone trade market is minuscule, it is also overcrowded, with the presence of all the 'big five' publishers, each of which run local publishing programmes alongside importing titles from the United States and the UK. Several of these publishers also function as distributors for smaller international independents; thus, for example, Penguin Random House India distributes books from Fitzcarraldo Editions and Sourcebooks, and HarperCollins India is the distributor for Oneworld and Harvard University Press, among others.[238] This means that, within a relatively small market sector, conglomerate publishers are responsible for three separate verticals: local publishing (with implications for the firms' local revenue targets), imports (with implications for the parent companies' revenue targets), and distributed titles (with implications for the companies' relationships with international players.) Conglomerate publishers' historic reliance on Amazon is perhaps understandable given the range of titles and the weak network of physical bookstores in the pre-pandemic years – while Amazon might not necessarily guarantee high visibility, it could at least promise availability across extensive front- and backlists.

Though the pandemic could not permanently alter Amazon's reach, across 2021 and 2022, the company made substantial changes to its operations, with repercussions for the publishing industry. This had a legal basis: during this time, the Competition Commission of India (CCI) opened investigations into Cloudtail. Cloudtail was a leading seller on Amazon India, with a characteristically complex ownership: it was run by Prione Business Services, itself a joint venture between Catamaran – an investment firm owned by prominent businessman Narayana Murthy (with a 76% stake) – and Amazon India, which owned the remaining 24%.[239] The ownership split

---

[238] See 'About Us', HarperCollins India; 'Penguin Random House India signs distribution agreements with UK-based Fitzcarraldo editions and US-based sourcebooks', Penguin India, 15 July, 2020.

[239] 'Amazon buys out Murthy Firm's stake in Cloudtail', *The Times of India*, December 23 2021.

was necessitated by laws preventing overseas companies 'from running an online retailer that holds inventory' – hence Amazon India's 'marketplace' model – but retailers complained that Cloudtail received preferential treatment on the platform, and was able to offer higher discounts.[240] In 2022, the joint venture was dissolved, and Amazon took over complete ownership; as a result, Cloudtail 'ceased its business-to-consumer operations'.[241] This was a boon to most of the retail sector, as Cloudtail had monopolised the online marketplace; but Cloudtail was also the seller favoured by most of the 'big five' publishers, and its loss meant that the logistical convenience and deep discounting of Amazon no longer held the same weight.[242] Instead, a return to several smaller marketplace sellers meant that the online bookselling space had become as fragmented as the physical one. Beyond this, as Amazon neared its tenth anniversary in the country, the company had begun to publicly declare its vision for the future – a vision that no longer prioritised bookselling. In 2023, Amazon announced a 'game plan' for India focusing on more investment in fashion, online groceries, and business-to-business solutions, with no mention of books.[243] And, despite their promises of growth, in 2023 Amazon declined to mention India in its first-quarter 'earnings call' for the first time since 2014, causing speculation about changing priorities in the region.[244] Ten years after Amazon India had grown to be the near-monopoly seller for books, then, a combination of legal restrictions and its own business priorities might make it appear less valuable to publishers.

Moreover, in 2022, Amazon India made a decision which dramatically affected Indian trade publishing – and, perhaps inadvertently, strengthened its bonds. On 1 February 2022, Amazon abruptly announced the

---

[240] Simon Goodley, 'Amazon fails to quash investigation into its Indian selling practices', *The Guardian*, 11 June 2021.

[241] 'Amazon's Cloudtail revenue declines by 84% to Rs 3,093 crore in FY23', *Business Standard*, 10 October 2023.

[242] See Sankar, 'What the pandemic means for this independent bookstore'.

[243] Naini Thaker, 'Inside Amazon's game plan for India', *Forbes India*, 3 October 2023.

[244] 'First time since 2014, Amazon omits India business from earnings call', *Business Standard*, 28 April 2023.

closure of Westland, the publishing company it had acquired in 2016; literary translator and book critic Arunava Sinha describes the trade's response as 'a concerted wail of despair across the English language publishing industry in general'.[245] The announcement was so sudden that books would have to be pulled off the shelves within the month; more bafflingly, it was not accompanied by any explanation, leaving the industry reeling. Westland was a well-respected, successful publisher, with 'a sizeable combination of sales volumes and cultural cache [sic]';[246] more to the point, Westland's legacy spanned a long history from its earliest days as a distributor, and the company had acquired 'tremendous goodwill across the publishing ecosystem' over the years.[247] The decision affected individuals and organisations across the field: experienced publishers and editors, bestselling authors, distributors, booksellers, and readers. Crucially, as the trade was left shaken by Amazon's decision, brick-and-mortar bookstores across the country stepped in to offer support. The *Times of India* reported that bookstores in Bengaluru offered higher discounts, reserved copies for customers, and even arranged for international shipping of Westland titles, and many booksellers emphasised Westland's iconic place in Indian publishing and book retail.[248] In fact, booksellers did not hesitate to take this opportunity to explicitly engage in independent bookseller activism. In an extended caption on Instagram, Champaca remarked of the decision:

> It is a reminder to all of us that we cannot expect a sense of responsibility from businesses like Amazon, for whom books are nothing more than a means to profit, for whom books are not vehicles of change, sites for solidarity. . . . Our

---

[245] Arunava Sinha, 'The forces behind Amazon's decision to shut-shop on Westland', *Open Axis*, 19 February 2022.

[246] Shrabonti Bagchi and Jayshree P. Upadhyay, 'What went wrong at Westland Books?', *Mint*, 5 February 2022.

[247] Ibid.

[248] 'As Westland chapter ends, many in Bengaluru rush to grab books', *The Times of India*, 5 February 2022.

> friends in other indie bookstores across India ... have articulated this as well. We urge you to support Westland authors and their books while you can, and buy independent.[249]

Similarly, bookseller Ravi Menezes invoked the power of the independent, suggesting that '[i]f Westland Books had remained independent, it might still have been around', and urging readers to '[p]atronise local bookstores or we all might go the Westland Books way'.[250] Luckily, Westland's closure had a happy ending; its publishing team set up an imprint under the same name with online platform Pratilipi in April 2022, and eventually republished many of its books under the new venture.[251] Nevertheless, the incident had undeniably altered ties within the industry; with Amazon's exit from Westland, their strongest link to the publishing field had disappeared, and the abruptness of their decision was an indication that while Amazon was seen by publishers as essential, the feeling was not mutual. At the same time, publishers were reminded of a set of players within the industry who could be relied on for support – the brick-and-mortar bookstore.

In offering this support, the brick-and-mortar bookstore was also better poised, post-pandemic, to meet publishers' needs. Thanks to their efforts across 2020 and 2021, many of these stores now had vibrant online presences and stronger delivery systems; The Book Shop, for example, proudly advertised on social media that they had delivered to every state in the country over the course of the pandemic.[252] Thus, conglomerate publishers

---

[249] Champaca Books (champacabooks), 'The business of publishing and selling books in India is a fraught one, and it was dealt a heavy blow this week with Amazon shutting down its publishing arm in India, Westland', Instagram, 3 February 2022.

[250] 'As Westland chapter ends'.

[251] Arunava Sinha, 'Westland Books: No sale, writing platform Pratilipi to start publishing venture with same team', *Scroll*, 1 April 2022.

[252] Chaturvedi and Narain, 'The many ways in which Delhi's The Bookshop reinvented itself'.

could rely on bookstores, for the first time, to provide some of the opportunities previously restricted to Amazon, such as the online pre-order. Bookstore pre-orders were demonstrably popular in post-pandemic years: in May 2023, Bookworm offered pre-orders of *Beyond the Story*, the biography of K-pop group BTS, and announced that all copies were reserved within two days.[253] Brick-and-mortar bookstores had always offered in-person events and author signings, but with more bookstores across the country – and more visibility for these bookstores – these advantages were even more apparent. For all these reasons, the post-pandemic logic of the field has seen conglomerate publishers turning – or returning – to the brick-and-mortar bookstore, and increasingly adopting the rhetoric of independent bookseller activism in urging readers to support their local bookstores. From 2021 onwards, Hachette India's FAQ page has listed the independent bookstores where their titles are available.[254] The reprioritisation extends beyond rhetoric to on-the-ground support; following their exclusive bookstore with Kunzum, Penguin Random House India announced a similar setup with The White Owl, Nagaland, in February 2024.[255] This is, perhaps, the beginning of new trend in collaboration between publishers and bookstores; it also underscores their ultimate interdependence in the wider context of trade publishing.

This complex relationship between bookstores' activism, Amazon's strategic decisions, and publishers' actions is a reminder that the revival of the brick-and-mortar bookstore is not the result of altruism, nor a reflection of some 'special' value inherent to books; rather, it is the result of a combination of rhetorical positioning, corporate priorities, and profit motives. The renewed status of the brick-and-mortar bookstore is both a result of bookstores' intentional, sustained activism post-pandemic and the decisions of corporate publishers, whose own needs – greater shelf-space for a wider selection of titles – might be better served, at least in the

---

[253] Bookworm Bookstore, Blr (bookworm_Kris). 'Thank you Armys for overwhelming response to the pre-order of BTS: Beyond the Story', X, 13 May 2023.

[254] 'FAQs', Hachette India.

[255] The White Owl (thewhiteowl_nagaland), 'Bigger and better, reimagined and rejuvenated!', Instagram, 8 February 2024.

immediate term, by the brick-and-mortar bookstore. Nevertheless, it remains evident that the combination of these factors has dramatically transformed the contemporary landscape of brick-and-mortar bookselling from a space of fragmentation, uncertainty, and marginalisation to one of possibility, expansion, and renewed bibliodiversity.

6 Conclusion

'Bookshops are not dying! In fact, did you know independent bookshops and chain bookshops are making a comeback?' begins a 2022 article in *All About Publishing* – a succinct illustration of the extraordinary changes in brick-and-mortar bookselling in India over the last decade, and a hopeful declaration of the end of the era of the 'death of the bookstore'.[256] Not even ten years since the threat of 'rapidly becoming an endangered species',[257] the field had transformed into a space where booksellers could proudly advertise that their shops were 'Open everyday [*sic*] and shipping everywhere', and big five publishers posted on social media to ask, 'How many of you are supporting your local independent bookstores?'[258] As I have attempted to illustrate over this Element, a set of complex, overlapping factors have worked together to explain this transformation in the field and its underlying logics. the 2000s and 2010s, brick-and-mortar bookstores were rendered vulnerable by the disorganisation, fragmentation, and lack of data within the industry: all factors which simultaneously advantaged e-retail companies like Amazon, thus further marginalising the bookstore. Bookstores faced added marginalisation in the form of the 'systemic lack of support shown by publishers' and others in the field.[259] With the onset of the COVID-19 pandemic, however, these factors began to change. Claire Squires remarks that the pandemic highlighted 'the longer-term infrastructural challenges of the publishing industry, including the amount of economic and algorithmic power developed and seized by Amazon';[260] crucially, in the Indian context, the pandemic served to briefly disrupt

---

[256] 'Bookshops are like private sanctuaries!', *All about Book Publishing*, 3 August 2022.

[257] Chandrasekaran, 'The death of the bookstore'.

[258] The Dogears Bookshop (the_dogears_bookshop), 'Just a reminder that you could gift a book this holiday season and we could help', Instagram, 17 December 2023; Penguin India (PenguinIndia), 'How many of you are supporting your local independent bookstores?', X, 27 July 2023.

[259] Chaturvedi and Narain, 'The many ways in which Delhi's The Bookshop reinvented itself'.

[260] Squires, 'Essential? Different? Exceptional?'

these elements of Amazon's power. In response, publishers were forced to reprioritise the physical bookstore; in parallel to this renewed support from the industry, bookstores began to expand their online presence, not just for sales, but also to engage in a form of independent bookseller activism aimed at cultivating support and solidarity from readers, authors, and the industry as a whole. The results have been a blossoming of brick-and-mortar bookstores across the country that has shown no signs of waning; at the time of writing, in August 2024, Bahrisons had just announced its expansion into a new city, Indore, and it seems likely that by the time of publication, the map of Indian bookstores would have expanded even further.[261]

What are the implications of this new life for the bookstore? The emergence of independent bookseller activism is perhaps the most visible transformation in the field, which had not seen any previous attempt at 'branding' the independent bookstore as a collective identity on this scale.[262] Now, bookstores across the country proudly describe themselves as 'an independently-owned ... bookstore and cafe, and a diverse community', an 'independent [bookstore] run by passionate booksellers (with slightly idiosyncratic reading tastes)', or a 'fiercely independent bookstore'.[263] The wider field, too, has seen more conversations about bookselling; in March 2024, for example, Simon & Schuster India launched a video series on Instagram called 'Women in the Book Trade', interviewing a set of booksellers – all of whom mention bookstores across the country, and cite each other as inspirations.[264] As a result, the bookselling field reflects the individual and collective identities of brick-and-mortar

---

[261] Bahrisons Booksellers (Bahrisons_booksellers), 'INDORE – We are in your city', Instagram, 16 August 2024. As predicted, at the time of editing, this statement holds true: both Bahrisons and Champaca have opened new outlets, amidst a host of other bookstores.

[262] See Miller, *Reluctant Capitalists*, for a discussion of 'branding' exercises such as 'Book Sense' in the USA.

[263] 'About Us', Champaca; 'Luna: The neighbourhood bookstore', Luna Books; Walking Bookfairs (walkingbookfairs), Instagram.

[264] Simon and Schuster India (simonandschusterin), 'In the lead up to International Women's Day, we are celebrating women in the Book Trade Week', Instagram, 5 March 2024.

bookstores across the country, as well as patterns of interdependence and mutual support within the industry – in a clear contrast to the impersonal algorithmic logics of Amazon. At the same time, greater visibility for the brick-and-mortar bookstore does not automatically negate the polarisation of the field, and despite improvements in sales, booksellers have continued to voice frustrations with Amazon's disproportionate power and the predatory pricing of e-commerce giants.[265] While the brick-and-mortar bookstore is undeniably in a far better position than pre-pandemic, and sales data from the Indian book market has been similarly promising, the lack of market regulation and legal protections are arguably the most pressing concern. The next few years will offer crucial insight into whether the renewed strength and visibility of the bookstore, accompanied by nascent trade associations such as the IBAI, might invest booksellers in the country with more power to organise and lobby for their interests to be maintained, irrespective of corporate and conglomerate priorities.

The world of Indian bookselling is under-researched, and its revitalisation offers several opportunities for further scholarship. Bookstores undoubtedly influence the broader field of publishing at every stage – from patterns in popular genres (with implications for acquisition and publishing decisions) to cultures of readership, browsing, and 'bookishness'.[266] While this Element has discussed the role of bookstores in promoting bibliodiversity, the example of series such as 'Women in the Book Trade' also points to the importance of considering diversity *within* the industry. On the one hand, by spotlighting independent or niche presses and marginalised voices, bookstores can resist becoming what bookseller Radhika Timbadia describes as 'a space of extreme privilege or an anodyne site of stationery-driven capitalism'[267] – but booksellers, like publishers,

---

[265] Venkatesh M Swamy, 'Why India's ookshops can thrive despite online giants only if publishers support them', *Scroll*, 6 March 2022.

[266] See Jessica Pressman, *Bookishness: Loving Books in a Digital Age* (New York: Columbia University Press, 2020).

[267] Timbadia, 'Bengaluru's Champaca Bookstore has worked out a model for surviving'.

operate with a 'curatorial paradigm',[268] and their gatekeeping function means that it is essential to examine and interrogate the dynamics of gender, class, and caste representation in the bookselling field.

As well, as discussed at the start of this Element, the publishing field in India is multiply diverse, and the focus of this Element forms part of a much larger landscape. Susan Hawthorne warns of the threat to bibliodiversity posed by 'recolonization';[269] while anglophone trade publishing in India is representative of many Indian writers and publishers, its linguistic context, as well as the dominance of multinational conglomerates in the space, must be acknowledged. The many other bookselling spaces within the country – which cater to local languages and diverse reading communities, and which have none of the corporate backing or level of organisation available to conglomerate publishing – are a key element of the overall bookselling landscape of the country, and its literary culture(s).[270] Equally important are the numerous initiatives that focus on making books available to the sizeable proportion of the country for whom the bookstore remains an unfamiliar, inaccessible, or unaffordable space, such as community libraries.[271] Alongside vital current research into 'informal' bookselling spaces such as the book bazaar, research into these spaces is necessary to fully understand the state of the book in contemporary India.

Bookselling is a field inherently characterised by rapid and constant change; and as the dramatic effects of COVID-19 have highlighted, it is

---

[268] Michael Bhaskar, 'Curation in publishing: Curatorial paradigms, filtering, and the structure of editorial choice', in *The Oxford Handbook of Publishing*, eds. Angus Phillips and Michael Bhaskar (Oxford: Oxford University Press, 2019), 226–43. For discussions on the role of booksellers in curation/selection, see also Josh Cook, *The Art of Libromancy*.

[269] Hawthorne, 'Bibliodiversity', 67.

[270] See, for example, Archita Raghu, 'Reimagining book stores: Neelam carves out space for anti-caste literature', *The New Indian Express*, 27 April 2023, for a description of a newly opened Tamil-language bookstore which stocks anti-caste literature 'not found in the ... Crosswords of the city and ... conveniently written out of history textbooks'.

[271] 'Publishing and the Pandemic' includes articles focusing on several of these initiatives, many formed during the pandemic.

impossible to predict what changes lie ahead, and how the bookselling landscape might further transform over the next decade. Nevertheless, at this present moment – nearly five years after the onset of the pandemic – the field seems alive with possibility. At the time of this writing, readers in India can have books delivered from stores across the country; sign up for a reading retreat with the theme of 'India in Translation', organised by Champaca; attend a 'bring your own book' book club at Dogears Bookshop, Goa; or join the recently launched Writing Club at The White Owl, Nagaland, which promises accountability – and high tea.[272] The transformation of the field that I have explored over this Element is, in many ways, only a beginning – it remains to be seen how these altered logics of brick-and-mortar bookselling in the country will affect the wider contexts of publishing in the years to come.

---

[272] Champaca Books (champacabooks), 'This September Champaca Bookstore is offering a reading retreat in Goa', Instagram, July 2024; The Dogears Bookshop (the_dogears_bookshop), 'After a hiatus of two months we are back!!', Instagram, 14 August 2024; The White Owl (thewhiteowl_nagaland), 'Join us for the launch of The White Owl's Writing Club', Instagram, 6 August 2024.

Bibliography

'About us'. Books at Bahri. Accessed 6 March 2024. www.booksatbahri.com/default.aspx?id=content&pid=aboutus.

'About us'. Bookshop.org. Accessed 6 March 2024. https://bookshop.org/info/about-us.

'About us'. Champaca. Accessed 6 March 2024. https://champaca.in/pages/about-us.

'About us'. HarperCollins India. Accessed 6 March 2024. https://harpercollins.co.in/about-us/.

'About us'. The Dogears Bookshop. Accessed 16 March 2024. www.thedogearsbookshop.com/about-us/.

'About us'. ThomsonPress. https://thomsonpress.com/about-us.html.

'About'. Kunzum. Accessed 6 March 2024. https://kunzum.com/about/.

Abraham, Thomas. 'After midnight: The English trade publishing scene'. *Logos* 33, no. 2–3 (December 2022): 28–37. https://doi.org/10.1163/18784712-03104037.

Abraham, Thomas. 'What can publishers, booksellers (and readers) do for the books business to recover after Covid-19?' *Scroll*, 25 April 2020. Accessed 5 March, 2024. https://scroll.in/article/959738/what-can-publishers-booksellers-and-readers-do-for-the-books-business-to-recover-after-covid-19.

Adams, Thomas R., and Nicolas Barker. 'A new model for the study of the book'. In *The Book History Reader*, edited by David Finkelstein and Alistair McCleery. 2nd ed., 47–65. London: Routledge, 2006.

Aditya, Harsh. 'Nine locations and one pandemic later, this independent bookstore still woos Patna's booklovers'. *Scroll*, 6 March 2021. https://scroll.in/article/988680/nine-locations-and-one-pandemic-later-this-independent-bookstore-still-woos-patnas-booklovers.

Alter, Alexandra, and Elizabeth A. Harris. 'Some surprising good news: Bookstores are booming and becoming more diverse'. *The New York Times*, 10 July 2022. www.nytimes.com/2022/07/10/books/bookstores-diversity-pandemic.html.

'Amazon buys out Murthy Firm's stake in Cloudtail'. *The Times of India*, December 23 2021. https://timesofindia.indiatimes.com/business/india-business/amazon-buys-out-murthy-firms-stake-in-cloudtail/articleshow/88442145.cms.

'Amazon launches first online shopping site in India'. *BBC*, 5 June 2013. www.bbc.com/news/business-22780571.

Amazon Staff. 'Amazon India strengthens its fulfilment and delivery network'. Amazon India, 1 October 2021. www.aboutamazon.in/news/operations/amazon-india-strengthens-its-fulfilment-and-delivery-network.

'Amazon's Cloudtail revenue declines by 84% to Rs 3,093 crore in FY23'. *Business Standard*, 10 October 2023. www.business-standard.com/india-news/amazon-s-cloudtail-revenue-declines-by-84-to-rs-3-093-crore-in-fy23-123101001263_1.html.

Anand, S. 'First person: How Navayana, publisher of anti-caste literature, was born, and where it is going now'. *Scroll*, 9 July 2020. https://scroll.in/article/966829/first-person-how-navayana-publisher-of-dalit-literature-was-born-and-where-it-is-going-now.

Ancheri, Saumya. 'Why Mumbai's iconic Strand Book Stall is shutting'. *Condé Nast Traveller India*, 22 February 2018. www.cntraveller.in/story/mumbais-iconic-strand-book-stall-shutting-next-week/.

Anderson, Porter. 'Coronavirus impact: Nielsen Book India on readers in the pandemic'. *Publishing Perspectives*, 15 July 2020. https://publishingperspectives.com/2020/07/coronavirus-impact-india-publishing-industry-nielsen-book-impact-study-pandemic-covid19/.

Anderson, Porter. 'Frankfurt week: A new report on the Indian book market'. *Publishing Perspectives*, 17 October 2022. https://publishingperspectives.com/2022/10/frankfurt-week-a-new-report-on-the-indian-market/.

'As Westland chapter ends, many in Bengaluru rush to grab books'. *The Times of India*, 5 February 2022. https://timesofindia.indiatimes.com/city/bengaluru/as-westland-chapter-ends-many-rush-to-grab-books/articleshow/89356369.cms.

Association of Publishers of India and EY-Parthenon. *Value Proposition of the India Publishing: Trends, Challenges, and the Future of the Industry | May 2021*. Ernst & Young, 2021. www.ey.com/en_in/strategy-transactions/the-now-next-and-beyond-of-the-indian-publishing-industry#:~:text=Value%20proposition%20of%20the%20Indian%20publishing&text=Print%20newspapers%20and%20magazines%20are,INR%20800%20billion%20by%202024.

Atta Galatta – The Bookstore (attagalatta). Instagram. Accessed 6 March, 2024. www.instagram.com/attagalatta/?hl=en.

Bagchi, Shrabonti, and Jayshree P. Upadhyay. 'What went wrong at Westland Books?' *Mint*, 5 February 2022. www.livemint.com/news/india/what-went-wrong-at-westland-books-11644074427112.html.

Bahrisons Bookseller (Bahrisons_books). 'Kolkata-We are in your town now!' X, 18 January 2023. Accessed 6 March 2024. https://twitter.com/Bahrisons_books/status/1615734662596558848?s=20.

Bahrisons Booksellers (Bahrisons_booksellers). 'An afternoon at Bahrisons'. Instagram, 20 May 2020. Accessed 6 March 2024. www.instagram.com/p/CAZeIuaJhJ1/?img_index=2.

Bahrisons Booksellers (Bahrisons_booksellers). 'Good news Delhi readers'. Instagram 11 May, 2020. Accessed 6 March 2024. www.instagram.com/p/CADV4iiJFsb/.

Bahrisons Booksellers (Bahrisons_booksellers). 'Hello readers'. Instagram, 26 July 2020. Accessed 6 March 2024. www.instagram.com/p/CDGYqIrpdxZ/?img_index=4.

Bahrisons Booksellers (Bahrisons_booksellers). '? INDORE – We are in your city'. Instagram, 16 August 2024. Accessed 19 August 2024. www.instagram.com/bahrisons_booksellers/p/C-t_0VGS30B/.

Bahrisons Booksellers (Bahrisons_booksellers). 'It's getting very warm in Delhi'. Instagram, 25 May 2020. Accessed 6 March 2024. www.instagram.com/p/CAmYxRCp87A/?igsh=MzRlODBiNWFlZA==.

Bahrisons Booksellers (Bahrisons_booksellers). 'Missing your favourite bookstore?' Instagram, 3 May 2020. Accessed 6 March 2024. www.instagram.com/p/B_uF1EUpIWK/.

Bahrisons Booksellers (Bahrisons_booksellers). 'More good news for Book Lovers!' Instagram, 4 May 2020. Accessed 6 March 2024. www.instagram.com/p/B_wjjv6JYbP/.

Bahrisons Booksellers (Bahrisons_booksellers). 'Thank you to all our customers and readers for all the love and support'. Instagram, 7 May 2020. Accessed 6 March 2024. www.instagram.com/p/B_4C_bdJXOZ/.

Bahrisons Booksellers (Bahrisons_booksellers). 'The news you have been waiting for'. Instagram, 1 June 2020. Accessed 6 March 2024. www.instagram.com/p/CA4pu8vJc5H/.

Bahrisons Booksellers (Bahrisons_booksellers). 'What are you reading-have you placed your order yet?' Instagram, 5 May 2020. Accessed 6 March 2024. www.instagram.com/p/B_zrsslppuR/.

Bahrisons Booksellers (Bahrisons_booksellers). Instagram. Accessed 6 March, 2024. www.instagram.com/bahrisons_booksellers/?hl=en.

'Become a member'. Independent Bookshops Association of India. Accessed 6 March 2024. www.indiebookshops.in/become-a-member/.

Bhaskar, Michael. 'Curation in publishing: Curatorial paradigms, filtering, and the structure of editorial choice'. In *The Oxford Handbook of Publishing*, edited by Angus Phillips and Michael Bhaskar, 226–243. Oxford: Oxford University Press, 2019.

Bhatt, Bhaskar. 'First person: How a publishing executive started helping migrant labourers during the lockdown'. *Scroll*, 21 June 2020. https://scroll.in/article/965212/first-person-how-a-publishing-executive-started-helping-migrant-labourers-during-the-lockdown.

'Bookshops'. Kunzum. Accessed 6 March 2024. https://kunzum.com/bookshops/.

'Bookshops are like private sanctuaries!' *All about Book Publishing*, August 3 2022. www.allaboutbookpublishing.com/9640/bookshops-are-like-private-sanctuaries/.

Bookworm Bookstore, Blr (bookworm_Kris). 'All independent bookstores like us get such questions'. X, 8 February 2022. Accessed 6 March 2024. https://twitter.com/bookworm_Kris/status/1491132955527286785?s=20.

Bookworm Bookstore, Blr (bookworm_Kris). 'Support independent bookstores'. X, 16 August 2021. Accessed 6 March 2024. https://twitter.com/bookworm_Kris/status/1427204360241520642?s=20.

Bookworm Bookstore, Blr (bookworm_Kris). 'Thank you Armys for overwhelming response to the pre-order of BTS: Beyond the Story'. X, 13 May 2023. Accessed 6 March 2024. https://twitter.com/bookworm_Kris/status/1657639905554472960?s=20.

Bourdieu, Pierre. 'The field of cultural production'. In *The Book History Reader*, edited by David Finkelstein and Alistair McCleery. 2nd ed., 99–120. London: Routledge, 2006.

Casa Kundera (casakundera). X. Accessed 6 March 2024. https://twitter.com/casakundera.

Champaca Books (champacabooks). 'As the public health crisis worsens . . . ' Instagram, 24 April 2021. Accessed 6 March,2024. www.instagram.com/p/COCSuUfpe2B/.

Champaca Books (champacabooks). 'Champaca is now delivering across India'. Instagram, 26 May 2020. Accessed 6 March 2024. www.instagram.com/p/CAo1UReptWE/.

Champaca Books (champacabooks). 'Champaca is open for pick-up'. Instagram, 4 May 2020. Accessed 6 March 2024. www.instagram.com/p/B_wOztRJlkx/.

Champaca Books (champacabooks). 'The bookshelves have appeared on the book wall!' Instagram, 6 May 2019. Accessed 6 March 2024. www.instagram.com/p/BxHjyWiJBvV/.

Champaca Books (champacabooks). 'The business of publishing and selling books in India is a fraught one, and it was dealt a heavy blow this week with Amazon shutting down its publishing arm in India, Westland'. Instagram, 3 February 2022. Accessed 6 March 2024. www.instagram.com/p/CZgpVeXqP0r/.

Champaca Books (champacabooks). 'This Diwali, meet the Champaca team'. Instagram, 14 November 2020. Accessed 6 March 2024. www.instagram.com/p/CHj_KlzJIlX/.

Champaca Books (champacabooks). 'This September Champaca Bookstore is offering a reading retreat in Goa'. Instagram, 23 July 2024. Accessed 19 August 2024. www.instagram.com/p/C9w9M78IPkk/?hl=en.

Champaca Books (champacabooks). 'We hope to see you for our online events in June'. Instagram, 3 June 2020. Accessed 16 March 2024. www.instagram.com/p/CA9tK51JJ8O/?igsh=MTZhOWk5YmpyZm82bg%3D%3D.

Champaca Books (champacabooks). 'We want to say a big and heartfelt thank you to everyone who has supported us through this lockdown!'

Instagram, 14 April 2020. Accessed 6 March 2024. www.instagram.com/p/B-80xVxJtZk/.

Champaca Books (champacabooks). 'We're branching out of our leafy home in Bangalore – and opening a bookstore in a new state!' Instagram, 25 October 2022. Accessed 6 March 2024. www.instagram.com/champacabooks/.

Champaca Books (champacabooks). 'We're terribly excited to announce our latest adventure'. Instagram, 7 June 2020. Accessed 6 March 2024. www.instagram.com/p/CBICPU8pvbs/.

Champaca Books (champacabooks). 'We've closed Champaca for a week till March 23rd'. Instagram, 19 March 2020. Accessed 6 March 2024. www.instagram.com/p/B96f9TkJSA2/.

Champaca Books (champacabooks). 'You can order books 📚 online from Champaca, your favourite independent bookstore'. Instagram, 21 February 2021. Accessed 6 March 2024. www.instagram.com/p/CLjLUJRJr8K/.

'Champaca Bookstore at Mahe, Goa'. Champaca. Accessed 6 March 2024. https://champaca.in/pages/champaca-goa.

Chandrasekaran, Kaavya. 'The death of the bookstore.' *Fortune India*, 5 July 2015. www.fortuneindia.com/technology/the-death-of-the-bookstore/100400.

Chandy, Anish. 'Why the pandemic will lead to a rush of new books on investment, personal finance and start-ups'. *Scroll*, 12 November 2020. https://scroll.in/article/977554/why-the-pandemic-will-lead-to-a-rush-of-new-books-on-investment-personal-finance-and-start-ups.

Charkin, Richard. 'Innovation, creativity and the unrealized potential of Indian trade publishing'. *Logos* 33, no. 2–3 (December 2022): 51–53. https://doi.org/10.1163/18784712-03104040.

Chaturvedi, Mahika, and Sonal Narain. 'The many ways in which Delhi's The Bookshop reinvented itself during the pandemic'. *Scroll*, 13 November

2020. https://scroll.in/article/978307/the-many-ways-in-which-delhis-the-bookshop-reinvented-itself-during-the-pandemic.

'Collections'. Champaca. Accessed 6 March 2024. https://champaca.in/collections.

'Collections'. Champaca. https://champaca.in/collections. Archived on 22 July 2020. Accessed via Internet Archive on 6 March 2024. https://web.archive.org/web/20200722022947/https://champaca.in/collections.

'Company Profile'. ReplikaPress. https://replikapress.com/company-profile.php.

Cook, Josh. *The Art of Libromancy: Selling Books and Reading Books in the Twenty-first Century*. Windsor: Biblioasis, 2023.

'Covid-19 lockdown: Government says no ban on inter-state movement of trucks'. *India Today*, 13 April 2020. www.indiatoday.in/india/story/covid-19-lockdown-government-says-no-ban-on-inter-state-movement-of-trucks-1666484-2020-04-13.

Crossword Bookstores (crossword_book). '100 stores, countless happy booklovers!' X, 8 September 2023. Accessed 6 March 2024. https://twitter.com/crossword_book/status/1700057475494658359?s=20.

D. Cruz, Beatriz Marie. 'Publishers, bookshops ride the digital wave spurred by pandemic'. *Business World*, 20 December 2023. www.bworldonline.com/top-stories/2023/12/20/564627/publishers-bookshops-ride-the-digital-wave-spurred-by-pandemic/.

D'Cruze, Danny. 'India's unique e-commerce story: Insights from Amazon India's VP on the last 10 years'. *Business Today*, 6 June 2023. Accessed 5 March 2024. www.businesstoday.in/technology/news/story/indias-unique-e-commerce-story-insights-from-amazon-indias-vp-on-the-last-10-years-384485-2023-06-06.

Darnton, Robert. 'What is the history of books?' *Daedalus* 111, no. 3 (1982): 65–83. www.jstor.org/stable/20024803.

Datta, Rohan. 'How Kolkata's famous Mohan's Bookshop lost its battle against the Covid-19 pandemic'. *Scroll*, 2 May 2021. https://scroll.in/article/993796/how-kolkatas-famous-mohans-bookshop-lost-its-battle-against-the-covid-19-pandemic.

De, Milinda. 'Sarat Book House: Bookselling, a noble profession'. *Logos* 33, no. 2–3 (December 2022): 69–73. https://doi.org/10.1163/18784712-03104042.

'Delhi's Khan Market world's 22nd priciest high street retail location'. *The Economic Times*, 22 November 2023. https://economictimes.indiatimes.com/industry/services/property-/-cstruction/delhis-khan-market-worlds-22nd-priciest-high-street-retail-location/articleshow/105395590.cms?from=mdr.

Deshpande, Sudhanva. 'Will the pandemic enable us to imagine our cities with more bookstores?' *Scroll*, 12 September 2020. https://scroll.in/article/972806/will-the-pandemic-enable-us-to-imagine-our-cities-with-more-bookstores.

Devasar, Nitasha. 'Why is Indian publishing not getting its due?' *All about Book Publishing*, 28 February 2020. www.allaboutbookpublishing.com/6829/why-is-indian-publishing-not-getting-its-due/.

Dhingra, Kanupriya, and Pritha Mukherjee. 'Bookselling in India: The "Proper" and the "Parallel"'. Presentation as part of the Bookselling Research Network, 26 January 2024.

Dhingra, Kanupriya. *Old Delhi's Parallel Book Bazaar*. Cambridge: Cambridge University Press, 2024.

'FAQs'. Hachette India. www.hachetteindia.com/Home/Faqs.

'First time since 2014, Amazon omits India business from earnings call'. *Business Standard*, 28 April 2023. www.business-standard.com/india-news/first-time-since-2014-amazon-omits-india-business-from-earnings-call-123042800322_1.html.

Ghosh, Sayantan. 'What we talk about when we talk about writing a novel during the pandemic'. *Scroll*, 20 June 2020. https://scroll.in/article/965113/what-we-talk-about-when-we-talk-about-writing-a-novel-during-the-pandemic.

Ghosh, Soma. 'On the death of a neighbour'. *The Times of India*, 10 July 2014. https://timesofindia.indiatimes.com/blogs/freeze-frame/death-of-a-bookshop/.

'Global book market 2024 shaped by strong fiction, declining non-fiction and slower price increases'. *Nielsen*, 15 October 2024. https://nielseniq.com/global/en/news-center/2024/global-book-market-2024-shaped-by-strong-fiction-declining-non-fiction-and-slower-price-increases/.

Goodley, Simon. 'Amazon fails to quash investigation into its Indian selling practices'. *The Guardian*, 11 June 2021. www.theguardian.com/technology/2021/jun/11/amazon-fails-to-quash-investigation-into-its-indian-selling-practices.

Govindarajan, Vijay, and Anita Warren. 'How Amazon adapted its business model to India'. *Harvard Business Review*, 20 July 2016. https://hbr.org/2016/07/how-amazon-adapted-its-business-model-to-india.

Greco, Albert N., Clara E. Rodríguez, and Robert M. Wharton. *The Culture and Commerce of Publishing in the 21st Century*. Stanford: Stanford University Press, 2007.

Griffin, Peter. 'Indie bookshops in India'. zigzackly's omnium-gatherum, 7 June 2022. Accessed 19 August 2024. https://zigzackly.blogspot.com/2022/06/indie-bookshops-in-india.html.

Gupta, Abhijit. 'The history of the book in the Indian subcontinent'. In *The Book: A Global History*, edited by Michael F. Suarez and H. R. Woudhuysen. 1st ed., 553–572. Oxford: Oxford University Press, 2013.

Gupta, Kanishka. 'Could the Coronavirus pandemic lock down Indian publishing for some time?' *Scroll*, 21 March 2020. https://scroll.in/

article/956676/could-the-coronavirus-pandemic-lock-down-indian-publishing-for-some-time.

Gupta, Kanishka. 'How a bookshop-in-mall chain learnt to stop worrying about, and start loving, the new normal'. *Scroll*, 30 October 2020. https://scroll.in/article/977086/how-a-bookshop-in-mall-chain-learnt-to-stop-worrying-about-and-start-loving-the-new-normal.

Gupta, Kanishka. 'How does the life of a book change as it goes from publisher to bookseller?' *Scroll*, 9 December 2017. https://scroll.in/article/860790/how-does-the-life-of-a-book-change-as-it-goes-from-publisher-to-bookseller.

Gupta, Kanishka. 'Six indie bookstores have founded an association of bookshops. What do they hope to achieve?' *Scroll*, 31 May 2020. https://scroll.in/article/963365/six-indie-bookstores-have-founded-an-association-of-bookshops-what-do-they-hope-to-achieve.

Haidar, Faizan. 'Bookstores look to turn the page, expand outlets'. *Economic Times*, 12 January 2023. https://m.economictimes.com/industry/services/property-/cstruction/bookstores-look-to-turn-the-page-expand-outlets/amp_articleshow/96920126.cms.

Harper Broadcast (HarperBroadcast). *#ShopTalk | Episode 1 | Shop around the Corner, Bahrisons Booksellers*. YouTube, 24 April 2020. Accessed 6 March 2024. www.youtube.com/watch?v=cQC2z4Q0N1g&list=PLCJvUW5Sl-w3X37A_r54zB8cSsvK-vTC2&index=6.

HarperCollins (HarperCollinsIN). 'We're so delighted that indie bookstores are opening slowly but surely'. X, 29 April 2020. Accessed 6 March 2024. https://twitter.com/HarperCollinsIN/status/1255441082277642241?s=20.

Hawthorne, Susan. 'Bibliodiversity: Creating content or invigorating culture?' *Logos* 27, no. 1 (June 2016): 63–71. https://doi.org/10.1163/1878-4712-11112099.

Hembrom, Ruby. 'Why the pandemic has made little difference to adivaani, Ruby Hembrom's Adivasi publishing house'. *Scroll*, 26 May 2020. https://scroll.in/article/962850/why-the-pandemic-has-made-little-difference-to-adivaani-ruby-hembroms-adivasi-publishing-house.

Highland, Kristen Doyle. *The Spaces of Bookselling: Stores, Streets, and Pages*. Cambridge: Cambridge University Press, 2023. doi:10.1017/9781108906500.

'Home'. Books at Bahri. www.booksatbahri.com/default.aspx. Archived on 8 October 2019. Accessed via Internet Archive on 6 March 2024. https://web.archive.org/web/20191008050741/http://www.booksatbahri.com/default.aspx.

'How it works'. Kunzum. Accessed 6 March 2024. https://kunzum.com/how-it-works/.

'I am trying to move away from Amazon and Audible for books since I find Amazon's work ethics questionable'. r/indianbooks. Reddit, 2020. Accessed 6 March 2024. www.reddit.com/r/Indianbooks/comments/ijcm4 t/i_am_trying_to_move_away_from_amazon_and_audible/.

'India Coronavirus: New record deaths as virus engulfs India'. *BBC*, 2 May 2021. www.bbc.com/news/world-asia-india-56961940.

'Is there an ethical place to buy books from?' r/indianbooks. Reddit, 2022. www.reddit.com/r/IndiansRead/comments/w7twgp/is_there_an_ethical_place_to_buy_books_from_i/.

John, Binoo K. 'Why bookshops are closing down when book-reading is thriving'. *Scroll*, 7 August 2015. https://scroll.in/article/746751/why-bookshops-are-closing-down-when-book-reading-is-thriving.

'Kanishka Gupta'. Publishers Marketplace. Accessed 6 March 2024. www.publishersmarketplace.com/members/writersside2010/.

Kapoor, Priya. 'For illustrated books, the lockdown makes production difficult. But a digital future brings hope'. *Scroll*, 15 May 2020. https://

scroll.in/article/961986/for-illustrated-books-the-lockdown-makes-production-difficult-but-a-digital-future-brings-hope.

Kapur, Mita. 'How do you run India's biggest literary prize, the JCB Prize for Literature, in a pandemic year?' *Scroll*, 20 December 2020. https://scroll.in/article/980711/how-do-you-run-indias-biggest-literary-prize-the-jcb-prize-for-literature-in-a-pandemic-year.

Karia, Vedant. 'STORY bookstore returns with a grand palatial look in Salt Lake'. *Telegraph*, 11 August 2023. www.telegraphindia.com/my-kolkata/events/storys-new-home-in-salt-lake-is-a-testament-to-its-prolific-legacy/cid/1958340.

Karia, Vedant. 'STORY opens doors in New Town'. *Telegraph*, 23 September 2023. www.telegraphindia.com/my-kolkata/places/story-opens-doors-in-new-town-photogallery/cid/1968345.

Kenyon, Hazel. 'Frankfurt Book Fair 2023: Tracking trends in international book sales'. *Publishers Weekly*, 19 October 2023. www.publishersweekly.com/pw/by-topic/international/Frankfurt-Book-Fair/article/93471-frankfurt-book-fair-2023-tracking-trends-in-international-book-sales.html.

Khan, Tarana Husain. 'The journey of the Rampur book club shows how reading communities responded to the pandemic'. *Scroll*, 20 August 2020. https://scroll.in/article/970843/the-journey-of-the-rampur-book-club-shows-how-reading-communities-responded-to-the-pandemic.

Kinder, Kimberley. *The Radical Bookstore: Counterspace for Social Movements*. Minneapolis: University of Minnesota Press, 2021.

Krocha, Vishü Rita. 'The Common Room, turning a new page amid the pandemic'. *Morung Express*, 14 September 2020. https://morungexpress.com/the-common-room-turning-a new page amid the pandemic.

'Kunzum Book Clubs'. Kunzum. Accessed 6 March, 2024. https://kunzum.com/bookclubs/.

Kuruganti, Sruthi. 'Here's a new place for bibliophiles in Hyderabad to explore'. *Telangana Today*, 27 October 2022. https://telanganatoday.com/heres-a-new-place-for-bibliophiles-in-hyderabad-to-explore.

Laing, Audrey, and Jo Royle. 'Bookselling culture and consumer behaviour: Marketing strategies and consumer responses in UK chain bookshops'. In *The Future of the Book in the Digital Age*, edited by Bill Cope and Angus Phillips, 115–134. Oxford: Chandos, 2006.

Laing, Audrey. 'Indies in Scotland: Exploring the unique role of independent bookshops in Scotland's towns and villages'. *Publishing Research Quarterly* 36, no. 4 (December 2020): 585–600. https://doi.org/10.1007/s12109-020-09759-5.

Le Roux, Elizabeth, Savannah Harvett, and Lezli Edgar. *South African Book Publishing Industry Survey 2022-23*. Cape Town: Publishers' Association of South Africa, 2024.

'Luna: the neighbourhood bookstore'. Luna Books. Accessed 6 March 2024. www.lunabooks.in.

MacTavish, Kenna. 'Crisis book browsing: Restructuring the retail shelf life of books'. In *Bookshelves in the Age of the COVID-19 Pandemic*, edited by Corinna Norrick-Rühl and Shafquat Towheed, 49–68. Cham: Springer International, 2022. https://doi.org/10.1007/978-3-031-05292-7_3.

Madhok, Karan. 'Will Mussoorie's Cambridge book depot open after the pandemic? Residents and visitors are hoping so'. *Scroll*, 6 June 2021. https://scroll.in/article/996746/will-mussoories-cambridge-book-depot-open-after-the-pandemic-residents-and-visitors-are-hoping-so.

Maitreya, Yogesh. 'How Panther's Paw publications is publishing its Dalit books during, and against, the pandemic'. *Scroll*, 4 August 2020. https://scroll.in/article/969353/how-panthers-paw-publications-is-publishing-its-dalit-books-during-and-against-the-pandemic.

Malhotra, Priyanka. 'The pandemic claims an iconic bookshop as Full Circle Bookstore in Delhi's Khan Market closes'. *Scroll*, 7 June 2020.

https://scroll.in/article/964043/the-pandemic-claims-an-iconic-bookshop-as-full-circle-bookstore-in-delhis-khan-market-closes.

Malhotra, Rajni Bahri, and Anuj Bahri Malhotra. 'What led Delhi's Bahrisons to open a new bookshop in the capital during the pandemic?' *Scroll*, 19 October 2020. https://scroll.in/article/976097/what-led-delhis-bahrisons-to-open-a-new-bookshop-in-the-capital-during-the-pandemic.

Malik, Priyanjali. 'Farewell to the Bookshop'. *The Wire*, 31 October 2023. https://thewire.in/books/farewell-to-the-bookshop.

Mallya, Vinutha. 'Amazon's Westland plan: Game-changing or gaming the book industry?' Leftword, 1 February 2022. https://mayday.leftword.com/blog/post/amazons-westland-plan-game-changing-or-gaming-the-book-industry.

Mallya, Vinutha. 'Nielsen values Indian publishing at $3.9 billion'. *Publishing Perspectives*, 21 October 2015. https://publishingperspectives.com/2015/10/nielsen-values-indian-publishing-at-3-9-billion/.

Manur, Anupam. 'Time to abolish the MRP'. *The Hindu*, 22 July 2015. www.thehindu.com/opinion/op-ed/maximum-retail-price-is-an-archaic-dysfunctional-mechanism/article7452745.ece.

Markou, Helena. 'The window of opportunity: Success and failure in UK bookselling'. *Logos* 34, no. 1 (September 2023): 7–23. https://doi.org/10.1163/18784712-03104055.

Mathur, Vikrant. 'Frankfurt Book Fair 2022: India's book market booms'. *Publishers Weekly*, 21 October 2022. www.publishersweekly.com/pw/by-topic/international/Frankfurt-Book-Fair/article/90699-frankfurt-book-fair-2022-india-s-book-market-booms.html.

Mazumdar, Arunima. 'Why Pagdandi of Pune transformed its library-cum-cafe into a bookstore during the pandemic'. *Scroll*, 1 August 2021. https://scroll.in/article/1001624/why-pagdandi-of-pune-transformed-its-library-cum-cafe-into-a-bookstore-during-the-pandemic.

Menon, Rashmi. 'Indie bookstores are turning the page'. *Mint*, October 8 2020. www.livemint.com/news/business-of-life/indie-bookstores-are-turning-the-page-11602164330639.html.

'MHA order and guidelines dated 1.5.2020 about extension of lock down beyond 4.5.2020'. Government of India Ministry of Home Affairs, 1 May 2020. Accessed 5 March, 2024. https://ndma.gov.in/sites/default/files/PDF/covid/MHA-Order-Dt.-1.5.2020-to-extend-Lockdown-period-for-2-weeks-w.e.f-4.5.2020-with-new-guidelines.pdf.

'MHA Order Dt. 30.5.2020 with guidelines on extension of LD in containment zones and phased reopening'. Government of India Ministry of Home Affairs, 30 May 2020. Accessed 5 March 2024. https://ndma.gov.in/sites/default/files/PDF/covid/MHAOrderDt_30052020.pdf.

Miller, Laura. *Reluctant Capitalists: Bookselling and the Culture of Consumption*. Chicago: University of Chicago Press, 2006.

Milliot, Jim. 'Following a successful 2023, B&N aims to open 50 stores in 2024'. *Publishers Weekly*, 10 January 2024. www.publishersweekly.com/pw/by-topic/industry-news/bookselling/article/94063-following-a-successful-2023-b-n-will-open-50-stores-in-2024.html.

Mishra, Satabdi. 'How did a travelling indie bookshop close down and then re-open in the middle of a pandemic?' *Scroll*, 25 November 2020. https://scroll.in/article/979344/how-did-a-travelling-indie-bookshop-close-down-and-then-re-open-in-the-middle-of-a-pandemic.

Murray, Simone. 'Publishing studies: Critically mapping research in search of a discipline'. *Publishing Research Quarterly* 22, no. 4 (December 2006): 3–25. https://doi.org/10.1007/s12109-007-0001-4.

Muse, Eben J. *Fantasies of the Bookstore*. Cambridge: Cambridge University Press, 2022. https://doi.org/10.1017/9781108646000.

Nath, Dipanita. 'Pune Inc: How a bookstore is taking on e-commerce giants by focussing on old-fashioned reading habits'. *Indian Express*, 8 November 2022. https://indianexpress.com/article/cities/pune/

pune-inc-bookstore-taking-on-e-commerce-giants-old-fashioned-reading-habits-8256047/.

'National Capital Region Planning Board'. Accessed 26 March 2024. https://ncrpb.nic.in/ncrconstituent.html.

'New in the city: Get booked'. *Indian Express*, 10 April 2022. https://indianexpress.com/article/cities/chandigarh/chandigarh-booksellers-coffee-books-7862903/.

Nguyen, Hoang Viet, Hiep Xuan Tran, Le Van Huy, et al. 'Online book shopping in Vietnam: The impact of the COVID-19 pandemic situation'. *Publishing Research Quarterly* 36, no. 3 (September 2020): 437–445. https://doi.org/10.1007/s12109-020-09732-2.

Noorda, Rachel, and Stevie Marsden. 'Twenty-first century book studies: The state of the discipline'. *Book History* 22, no. 1 (2019): 370–97. https://muse.jhu.edu/pub/1/article/736560.

Noronha, Frederick. 'Publishing in the pandemic from a small state: How Goa, 1556 is trying to change the game'. *Scroll*, 17 November 2020. https://scroll.in/article/978675/publishing-in-the-pandemic-from-a-small-state-how-goa-1556-is-trying-to-change-the-game.

Norrick-Rühl, Corinna. *Book Clubs and Book Commerce*. Cambridge: Cambridge University Press, 2019. https://doi.org/10.1017/9781108597258.

Om Book Shop (ombookshop). 'Our first ever book shop in West Delhi'. Instagram, 22 December 2023. Accessed 4 March 2024. www.instagram.com/p/C1KHH34yhNd/?utm_source=ig_web_copy_link&igsh=ODhhZWM5NmIwOQ%3D%3D.

Pagdandi Bookstore Café (pagdandi). 'The reading circle is back at Pagdandi!' Instagram, 13 September 2023. Accessed 6 March 2024. www.instagram.com/p/CxILDk-IfkW/?utm_source=ig_web_copy_link.

Panchal, Salil, and Deepti Chaudhary. 'The new digital newsroom'. *Forbes India*, 31 August 2016. www.forbesindia.com/article/big-bet/the-new-digital-newsroom/44139/1.

Pant, Meghna. 'How to get published during the pandemic and afterwards (warning: It will not be easy)'. *Scroll*, 2 December 2020. https://scroll.in/article/979829/how-to-get-published-during-the-pandemic-and-afterwards-warning-it-will-not-be-easy.

Parakala, Vangmayi. 'Westland's Gautam Padmanabhan: The comeback man'. *Mint*, 28 July 2023. https://lifestyle.livemint.com//news/big-story/westland-pratilipi-gautam-padmanabhan-amazon-book-publishing-indian-publishers-111690480103250.html.

Penguin India (PenguinIndia). 'Good news for those of you who need to breathe in the new-book smell of paper and ink!' X, 2 May 2020. Accessed 6 March 2024. https://twitter.com/PenguinIndia/status/1256515064825176064?s=20.

Penguin India (PenguinIndia). 'How many of you are supporting your local independent bookstores?' X, 27 July 2023. Accessed 6 March 2024. https://twitter.com/PenguinIndia/status/1684598050025824256.

'Penguin Random House India signs distribution agreements with UK-based Fitzcarraldo editions and US-based Sourcebooks'. Penguin India, 15 July 2020. www.penguin.co.in/newsroom/penguin-random-house-india-signs-distribution-agreements-with-uk-based-fitzcarraldo-editions-and-us-based-sourcebooks/.

Politi, Daniel. 'Through a recession and a pandemic, the book business is thriving in Buenos Aires'. *The New York Times*, 26 May 2022. www.nytimes.com/2022/05/26/books/buenos-aires-books.html#:~:text=New%20York%20Times-,Through%20a%20Recession%20and%20a%20Pandemic%2C%20the%20Book%20Business%20Is,residents%20in%20fresh%20reading%20material.

Pressman, Jessica. *Bookishness: Loving Books in a Digital Age*. New York: Columbia University Press, 2020.

Punj, Shweta, Anilesh S. Mahajan, M. G. Arun, and Kiran Tare. 'Meeting the demand for supply'. *India Today*, 13 April 2020. www.indiatoday.in/magazine/cover-story/story/20200413-meeting-the-demand-for-supply-1662861-2020-04-04.

Purohit, Manish. 'As publishers face challenges, will self-publishing actually become bigger after the pandemic?' *Scroll*, 10 June 2020. https://scroll.in/article/964252/as-publishers-face-challenges-will-self-publishing-actually-become-bigger-after-the-pandemic.

Raghu, Archita. 'Reimagining book stores: Neelam carves out space for anti-caste literature'. *The New Indian Express*, April 27 2023. www.newindianexpress.com/cities/chennai/2023/Apr/27/reimagining-book-stores-neelam-carves-out-space-for-anti-caste-literature-2569697.html.

Ray Murray, Padmini, Rashmi Dhanwani, and Kavya Iyer Ramalingam. *India literature and publishing sector study | December 2020 – May 2021*. British Council, 2021. Accessed 5 March, 2024. www.britishcouncil.in/programmes/arts/india-literature-and-publishing-sector-study.

Rosen, Judith. 'The changing world of bookselling'. *Publishers Weekly*, 19 April 2022. www.publishersweekly.com/pw/by-topic/industry-news/bookselling/article/89023-the-changing-world-of-bookselling.html.

Sahay, Manjari. 'Independent bookshops: What the lockdown, Covid-19 and its aftermath may mean for them'. *Scroll*, 8 May 2020. https://scroll.in/article/961278/independent-bookshops-what-the-lockdown-covid-19-and-its-aftermath-may-mean-for-them.

Sankar, Subodh. 'What the pandemic means for this independent bookstore which thrives on its physical space'. *Scroll*, 22 August 2020. https://scroll.in/article/970971/what-the-pandemic-means-for-this-independent-bookstore-which-thrives-on-its-physical-space.

Scroll Staff. 'Insider predictions: What does the future of publishing look like after the pandemic?' *Scroll*, 4 January 2021. https://scroll.in/article/983020/insider-predictions-what-does-the-future-of-publishing-look-like-after-the-pandemic.

Sheth, Selina. 'How this children's publisher defied the downtrend to boost sales during the pandemic'. *Scroll*, 22 August 2021. https://scroll.in/article/1003398/how-this-childrens-publisher-defied-the-downtrend-to-boost-sales-during-the-pandemic.

Sheth, Selina. 'Mumbai's elegantly curated Wayword & Wise bookshop refuses to go online despite the pandemic. Why?' *Scroll*, 15 November 2020. https://scroll.in/article/978522/mumbais-elegantly-curated-wayword-wise-bookshop-refuses-to-go-online-despite-the-pandemic-why.

Sheth, Selina. 'Walden, Hyderabad (1990–2020): The bookshop that, sadly, could not survive the pandemic'. *Scroll*, 6 December 2020. https://scroll.in/article/980374/walden-hyderabad-1990-2020-the-bookshop-that-sadly-could-not-survive-the-pandemic.

Simon and Schuster India (simonandschusterin). 'In the lead up to International Women's Day, we are celebrating women in the book trade week'. Instagram, 5 March 2024. Accessed 17 March 2024. www.instagram.com/reel/C4H4ZJwLdUR/?hl=en.

Singh, Ajit Vikram. 'A former bookseller explains why bookshops will find the post-pandemic period especially difficult'. *Scroll*, 30 July 2020. https://scroll.in/article/968923/a-former-bookseller-explains-why-bookshops-will-find-the-post-pandemic-period-especially-difficult.

Sinha, Arunava. 'The forces behind Amazon's decision to shut-shop on Westland'. *Open Axis*, 19 February 2022. https://openaxis.in/2022/02/19/4274/.

Sinha, Arunava. 'Westland books: No sale, writing platform Pratilipi to start publishing venture with same team'. *Scroll*, 1 April 2022. https://

scroll.in/article/1020816/westland-books-no-sale-writing-platform-pratilipi-to-start-publishing-venture-with-same-team.

Soofi, Mayank Austen. 'Delhiwale: The Khan Market matriarch'. *Hindustan Times*, 15 July 2019. www.hindustantimes.com/delhi-news/delhiwale-the-khan-market-matriarch/story-BHrmQapW7E6g8dRtKnlFlK.html.

Squires, Claire. 'Essential? Different? Exceptional? The book trade and Covid-19'. *C21 Literature: Journal of 21st-Century Writings* 9, no. 1 (2022). https://doi.org/10.16995/c21.3447.

Steiner, Ann. 'Select, display, and sell: Curation practices in the bookshop'. *Logos* 28, no. 4 (March 2017): 18–31. https://doi.org/10.1163/1878-4712-11112138.

Storyteller Bookstore (Storytellerkol). 'As independent bookshops, one has no leverage and has to always be at the mercy of book suppliers'. X, 15 August 2021. Accessed 6 March 2024. https://twitter.com/StorytellerKol/status/1426836936820330496?s=20.

Striphas, Ted. *The Late Age of Print: Everyday Book Culture from Consumerism to Control*. New York: Columbia University Press, 2009.

Sundaram, Mythili, and Ram Sarangan. 'How to open a new bookshop during the pandemic: The story of Sudarsan Books of Nagercoil'. *Scroll*, 22 December 2020. https://scroll.in/article/981947/how-to-open-a-new-bookshop-during-the-pandemic-the-story-of-sudarsan-books-of-nagercoil.

'Support independent bookshops'. r/indianbooks. Reddit, 2022. Accessed 6 March 2024. www.reddit.com/r/Indianbooks/comments/rvsuwg/support_independent_bookshops/.

Swamy, Venkatesh M. 'Why India's bookshops can thrive despite online giants only if publishers support them'. *Scroll*, 6 March 2022. https://scroll.in/article/1018600/why-indias-bookshops-can-thrive-despite-online-giants-only-if-publishers-support-them.

Thaker, Naini. 'Inside Amazon's game plan for India'. *Forbes India*, 3 October 2023. www.forbesindia.com/article/take-one-big-story-of-the-day/inside-amazons-game-plan-for-india/88633/1.

Thatipalli, Mallik. 'Low costs, moderate hopes: How Hyderabad's last independent bookstore is trying to survive Covid-19'. *Scroll*, 15 October 2020. https://scroll.in/article/975788/low-costs-moderate-hopes-how-hyderabads-last-independent-bookstore-is-trying-to-survive-covid-19.

Thayer, Winter M., Md Zabir Hasan, Prithvi Sankhla, and Shivam Gupta. 'An interrupted time series analysis of the lockdown policies in India: A national-level analysis of COVID-19 incidence'. *Health Policy and Planning* 36, no. 5 (June 3, 2021): 620–629. https://doi.org/10.1093/heapol/czab027.

'The book desert map'. Unite for Literacy. Accessed 5 March 2024. www.unitebooks.com/book-deserts/the-book-desert-map.

'The Champaca children's library'. Champaca. Accessed 6 March 2024. https://champaca.in/pages/library.

The Common Room (__thecommonroom__). Instagram. Accessed 6 March 2024. www.instagram.com/__thecommonroom__/?hl=en.

The death of Mumbai's strand book stall'. *Rediff*, 2 March 2018. www.rediff.com/getahead/report/books-the-death-of-a-bookstore-strand-book-stall-mumbai-shuts-down/20180302.htm.

The Dogears Bookshop (the_dogears_bookshop). 'After a hiatus of two months we are back!!'. Instagram, 14 August 2024. Accessed 19 August 2024. www.instagram.com/p/C-pdNDANM8S/?hl=en.

The Dogears Bookshop (the_dogears_bookshop). 'Just a reminder that you could gift a book this holiday season and we could help'. Instagram, 17 December 2023. Accessed 17 March 2024. www.instagram.com/the_dogears_bookshop/p/C09jcnktuSN/?hl=en.

The Dogears Bookshop (the_dogears_bookshop). 'Putting this out here'. Instagram, 22 January 2024. Accessed 6 March 2024. www.instagram.com/p/C2ZRc6iIv-a/?utm_source=ig_web_copy_link.

The Dogears Bookshop (the_dogears_bookshop). Instagram. Accessed 6 March 2024. www.instagram.com/the_dogears_bookshop/?hl=en.

The White Owl (thewhiteowl_nagaland). 'Bigger and better, reimagined and rejuvenated!' Instagram, 8 February 2024. Accessed 6 March 2024. www.instagram.com/p/C3E4oFfvkii/.

The White Owl (thewhiteowl_nagaland). 'Join us for the launch of The White Owl's Writing Club'. Instagram, 6 August 2024. Accessed 19 August 2024. www.instagram.com/p/C-VUUEBP6qM/.

'The white owl literature festival & book fair: A literary extravaganza in the heart of Nagaland'. The White Owl. Accessed 6 March, 2024. https://thewhiteowl.in/index.php/2024/01/09/white-owl-literature-festival/.

Thomas, Niels Peter. 'Bookselling'. In *The Oxford Handbook of Publishing*, edited by Angus Phillips and Michael Bhaskar, 399–408. Oxford: Oxford University Press, 2019.

Thompson, John B. *Merchants of Culture: The Publishing Business in the Twenty-First Century*. Newark: Polity Press, 2013.

Timbadia, Radhika. 'Bengaluru's Champaca Bookstore has worked out a model for surviving the pandemic and its aftermath'. *Scroll*, 6 August 2020. https://scroll.in/article/969533/bengalurus-champaca-bookstore-has-worked-out-a-model-for-surviving-the-pandemic-and-its-aftermath.

Vaidya, Abhay. 'The death of a bookstore: Why Pune's Twistntales is closing down'. *Firstpost*, February 23 2013. www.firstpost.com/living/the-death-of-a-bookstore-why-punes-twistntales-is-closing-down-636880.html.

Vergara, Trini. 'Frankfurt book fair 2023: Brazil's Skeelo looks to go global'. *Publishers Weekly*, 20 October 2023. www.publishersweekly

.com/pw/by-topic/international/Frankfurt-Book-Fair/article/93487-frankfurt-book-fair-2023-brazil-s-skeelo-looks-to-go-global.html.

Walking Book Fairs (walkingbookfairs). Instagram. Accessed 6 March 2024. www.instagram.com/walkingbookfairs/?hl=en.

Walking Bookfairs (walkingbookfairs). 'We made a beautiful new bookstore for you'. Instagram, October 2 2023. Accessed 6 March 2024. www.instagram.com/reel/Cx4l2_4yE61/?utm_source=ig_web_copy_link&igsh=MzRlODBiNWFlZA%3D%3D.

'Who we are'. The White Owl. Accessed 6 March 2024. https://thewhiteowl.in/index.php/who-we-are/.

Wolf, Gita. 'For Tara Books, maker of handmade books, the road to sustenance in the pandemic has not been easy'. *Scroll*, 10 November 2020. https://scroll.in/article/978092/for-tara-press-maker-of-handmade-books-the-road-to-sustenance-in-the-pandemic-has-not-been-easy.

Wood, Heloise. 'BA describes "volatile year" for bookshop openings and closures'. *The Bookseller*, 5 January 2024. www.thebookseller.com/news/ba-describes-volatile-year-for-bookshop-openings-and-closures.

World Intellectual Property Organization. *The Global Publishing Industry in 2022*. Geneva: WIPO, 2023. https://doi.org/10.34667/TIND.48714.

Acknowledgements

I would like to thank Samantha Rayner and Eben Muse for the opportunity to publish in this series, as well as the anonymous peer reviewers for their detailed and generous feedback. I am also grateful to the organisers of the Bookselling Research Conference in 2023, where I presented early stages of this research. This Element is based on the thesis I wrote as part of my MA degree at the University of Münster, and I am immeasurably grateful to Prof Dr Corinna Norrick-Rühl and Ellen Barth for their supervision, and for constant support and encouragement.

My interest in bookselling was shaped by my own experiences working in publishing in India, and I am indebted to everyone I worked with during this time, especially those in the sales and product teams, who were so generous with their time and experience, and helped me decode a field that often seemed to have very little logic. I am also grateful to the many incredible booksellers who worked throughout the pandemic, sharing photos of new releases and in some cases personally delivering orders.

Thank you to Chandni Ananth, Chiara Bullen, and Ash Jayamohan for feedback and support. Thank you to my family: Nirica, in her professional capacity as an independent bookseller, and her personal one as my sister; my mother, who made sure I had *You've Got Mail* and *84, Charing Cross Road* memorised at a formative age; and my father, who took us to the bookstore every weekend.

And, finally, to two bookstores which no longer exist: Bookends, Cisons Complex, Chennai, whose legacy lives on in tattered library cards on the family bookshelves; and Landmark, Apex Plaza, Chennai, where I spent a blissful childhood learning to know and love the business of books.

Cambridge Elements ≡

Publishing and Book Culture

SERIES EDITOR
Samantha J. Rayner
University College London

Samantha J. Rayner is Professor of Publishing and Book Cultures at UCL. She is also Director of UCL's Centre for Publishing, co-Director of the Bloomsbury CHAPTER (Communication History, Authorship, Publishing, Textual Editing and Reading), and co-Chair of the Bookselling Research Network.

ASSOCIATE EDITOR
Leah Tether
University of Bristol

Leah Tether is Professor of Medieval Literature and Publishing at the University of Bristol. With an academic background in medieval French and English literature and a professional background in trade publishing, Leah has combined her expertise and developed an international research profile in book and publishing history from manuscript to digital.

ADVISORY BOARD

Simone Murray, Monash University
Claire Squires, University of Stirling
Andrew Nash, University of London
Leslie Howsam, Ryerson University
David Finkelstein, University of Edinburgh
Alexis Weedon, University of Bedfordshire
Alan Staton, Booksellers Association
Angus Phillips, Oxford International Centre for Publishing
Richard Fisher, Yale University Press
John Maxwell, Simon Fraser University
Shafquat Towheed, The Open University
Jen McCall, Central European University Press/Amsterdam University Press

About the Series

This series aims to fill the demand for easily accessible, quality texts available for teaching and research in the diverse and dynamic fields of Publishing and Book Culture. Rigorously researched and peer-reviewed Elements will be published under themes, or 'Gatherings'. These Elements should be the first check point for researchers or students working on that area of publishing and book trade history and practice: we hope that, situated so logically at Cambridge University Press, where academic publishing in the UK began, it will develop to create an unrivalled space where these histories and practices can be investigated and preserved.

Cambridge Elements

Publishing and Book Culture

Bookshops and Bookselling

Gathering Editor: Eben Muse

Eben Muse is Senior Lecturer in Digital Media at Bangor University and co-Director of the Stephen Colclough Centre for the History and Culture of the Book. He studies the impact of digital technologies on the cultural and commercial space of bookselling, and he is part-owner of a used bookstore in the United States.

ELEMENTS IN THE GATHERING

Digital Authorship: Publishing in the Attention Economy
Lyle Skains

Capital Letters: The Economics of Academic Bookselling
J. M. Hawker

Book Clubs and Book Commerce
Corrina Norrick-Rühl

London and the Modernist Bookshop
Matthew Chambers

Fantasies of the Bookstore
Eben J. Muse

The Spaces of Bookselling: Stores, Streets, and Pages
Kristen Doyle Highland

Reading Spaces in Modern Japan: The Evolution of Sites and Practices of Reading
Andrew T. Kamei-Dyche

Selling Books with Algorithms
Anna Muenchrath

Old Delhi's Parallel Book Bazaar
Kanupriya Dhingra

Women Booksellers in the Twentieth Century: Hidden Behind the Bookshelves
Samantha J. Rayner

The Brick-and-Mortar Bookstore in Contemporary India
Nayantara Srinivasan

A full series listing is available at: www.cambridge.org/EPBC

Printed by Integrated Books International,
United States of America